LARRY SANG'S

CHINESE ASTROLOGY & FENG SHUI GUIDE

2014

The Year of The Horse

with Lorraine Wilcox

LARRY SANG'S

The Year of The Horse
ASTROLOGY AND FENG SHUI GUIDE

Original Title:
Master Larry Sang's 2014 The Year of the Horse, Astrology and Feng Shui Guide

Published by: The American Feng Shui Institute
7220 N. Rosemead Blvd., Suite 204
San Gabriel, CA 91775
Email: fsinfo@amfengshui.com
www.amfengshui.com

Written by:
Master Larry Sang

Edited by:
Lorraine Wilcox

Cover Design & Illustration by:
Afriany Simbolon

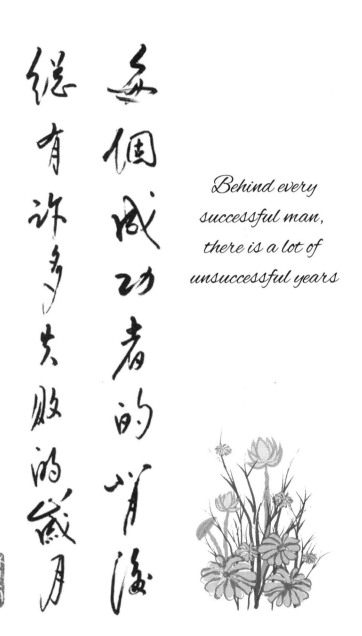

每個成功者的背後
總有許多失敗的歲月

Behind every successful man, there is a lot of unsuccessful years

Calligraphy by Larry Sang

Please Read This Information

This book provides information regarding the subject matter covered. The authors are not engaged in rendering legal, medical or other professional advice. If you need medical or legal advice, a competent professional should be contacted. Chinese Astrology and Feng Shui are not get-rich-quick or cure-all schemes. Changes in your life will happen as fast as you are ready for them. Be patient in your study of Chinese Astrology and Feng Shui.

The authors have tried to make this book as complete and accurate as possible. However, there may be typographical or content mistakes. Use this book as a general guide in your study of Chinese Astrology and Feng Shui.

This book was written to educate and entertain. The authors, distributors and the American Feng Shui Institute shall have neither liability nor responsibility to any person with respect to any loss or damage caused, or alleged to be caused by this book.

The following pages of predictions will help you understand trends as they develop through the coming year. Please keep in mind that they are somewhat general because other stellar influences are operative, according to the month, date and exact minute of your birth. Unfortunately, we cannot deal with each person individually in this book.

Table of Contents

How to find Your Animal Sign

In order to find your correct animal sign, as well as understand why the Chinese calendar begins in February, and not January, it is important to have a little understanding of the two different Chinese calendars. As with most things Chinese, we look at the Yin and Yang. In Chinese timekeeping, there is a Yin Calendar (Lunar calendar) and a Yang Calendar (Solar calendar).

The Lunar Calendar

The Lunar calendar is perhaps the best known and most popular of the two. Chinese Lunar New Year is frequently celebrated with a lot of pageantry. It is used in one type of Chinese Astrology called Zi Wei Dou Shu, and also in Yi Jing calculations.

The Solar Calendar

The Solar calendar is less well known. The early Chinese meteorologists attempts to gain insight into the cycles of the seasons. From this study, this developed the Solar calendar. This calendar is used in the form of Chinese Astrology called Four Pillars, as well as in Feng Shui. The Chinese were very accurate in their studies. Without computers, and using only observations, they mapped a solar year of 365 days. They missed the actual timing of a year by only 14 minutes and 12 seconds.

The solar year is divided into 24 solar terms. Each lasts about fifteen days. Spring Begins (lichun) is the name of the first day of Spring, and the first solar term. It is exactly midway between the winder solstice and the spring equinox. This is why it always falls on February 4th or 5th. We begin the five elements with wood, so the Chinese New Year begins with a wood month, whether in the Lunar or the Solar calendar. These concepts are derived from the Yi Jing.

愛情不是索取
而是給予

Love is giving,
not receiving

Calligraphy by Larry Sang

How to find your Animal Sign

To find your animal sign, start with your birth date. If it is before February 4th (Spring Begins), use the prior year for the Chinese calendar. If it is after February 4th, then use the same birth year. If it is on February 4th, then you need the time of the birth to accurately determine the birth animal. This information is contained in the Chinese Ten-Thousand Year Calendar. (The American Feng Shui institute has one available as an ebook at www.amfengshui.com). In the following pages, the birth years are listed for each animal, but remember, if your birthday is before February 4th, use the previous year to determine the animal.

The Twelve Animals

Rat 鼠	Ox 牛	Tiger 虎	Rabbit 兔
1924, 1936, 1948, 1960, 1972, 1984, 1996, 2008	1925, 1937, 1949, 1961, 1973, 1985, 1997, 2009	1926, 1938, 1950, 1962, 1974, 1986, 1998, 2010	1927, 1939, 1951, 1963, 1975, 1987, 1999, 2011
Dragon 龍	Snake 蛇	Horse 馬	Sheep 羊
1928, 1940, 1952, 1964, 1976, 1988, 2000, 2012	1929, 1941, 1953, 1965, 1977, 1989, 2001, 2013	1930, 1942, 1954, 1966, 1978, 1990, 2002, 2014	1931, 1943, 1955, 1967, 1979, 1991, 2003
Monkey 猴	Rooster 雞	Dog 狗	Pig 豬
1932, 1944, 1956, 1968, 1980, 1992, 2004	1933, 1945, 1957, 1969, 1981, 1993, 2005	1934, 1946, 1958, 1970, 1982, 1994, 2006	1935, 1947, 1959, 1971, 1983, 1995, 2007

FORTUNES OF THE 12 ANIMALS

The Horse

Note: The New Year begins February 4ᵗʰ

A brilliant money star, the Golden Cabinet, shines in your Ming Palace, so 2014 is a particularly rewarding year for the Horse. In career, the Horse's natural leadership and charisma are enhanced. You may find your ideas and initiatives get more traction than usual. The best strategy is to cultivate flexibility. Even though you meet with a lot of pressure and competition in your work, luck is on your side. Career and money prospects are at their best during the summer and early autumn. Lucrative opportunities should present themselves, especially to those born between the 4th of February and the 6th of March, but guard against greed. Don't push your luck on risky investments. Money luck is extremely strong in this year, but there are signs of financial mishaps taking place if you venture abroad. Salaried workers may discover a new source of income. Stress and insomnia are two health problems you should watch out for; also be careful of cuts as it will be easy to have some kind of bleeding. Be careful of falling from high places and accidents while traveling. Where romance is concerned, the single Horse may experience mood swings, but it will be exciting! Married Horses tend to be temperamental, so frequent squabbles may take place. To prevent a break up, control your temper and think twice before you act.

Your Benefactor is: Horse
(1930, 1942, 1954, 1966, 1978, 1990, 2002, 2014)

12 Month Outlook For The Horse

Solar Month	Comments
1st Month Feb 4th - Mar 5th	Though there is pressure on your job, money and career are looking good.
2nd Month Mar 6th - Apr 4th	Auspicious stars shine above! Opportunities will come knocking at your door.
3rd Month Apr 5th - May 4th	Luck is mixed between good and bad. Keep alert and do not take any risks if you are doubtful.
4th Month May 5th - Jun 5th	Pay attention to your health in order to avoid minor illness.
5th Month Jun 6th - Jul 6th	Average luck. You are busy physically and mentally.
6th Month Jul 7th - Aug 6th	Luck is smooth. Working hard enables you to strive for the best results.
7th Month Aug 7th - Sep 7th	It is easy to experience conflict and disharmony. Be less social and stay away from gossip.
8th Month Sep 8th - Oct 7th	A very auspicious time for you to plan something new or switch jobs.
9th Month Oct 8th - Nov 6th	Backstabbers are around. You are easily caught in squabbles.
10th Month Nov 7th - Dec 6th	Auspicious luck. Matters turn out well in nearly all aspects.
11th Month Dec 7th - Jan 5th	Luck is neither auspicious nor inauspicious.
12th Month Jan 6th - Feb 3rd	It is a good time to study or to learn something new.

The Sheep

1931, 1943, 1955, 1967, 1979, 1991, 2003

Note: The New Year begins February 4th

The male Sheep sees opportunities this year! You can take a big step forward in your career. The wind will be at your back during the Year of the Horse - whatever you want will come easily to you. Grab the opportunities and work hard. A plan put into motion toward the end of last year is beginning to reap rewards for you. Your good money prospects enable your savings to grow, due to the auspicious star named Tai Yang shining above. However, it is a year of mixed fortune for the female Sheep. Do not rush into things. If you are patient and calm and take one step at a time toward your goal, something will be obtained. Do not rush or act irrationally; otherwise it is likely you will encounter difficulties and danger. Avoid gambling or financial speculation or else it will be a losing game. Health-wise, frequent bouts of moodiness and depression may lead to insomnia. Those born in 1967 and 1955 should refrain from overworking lest they be stricken by illness. Where romance is concerned, a fruitful relationship awaits the male Sheep. Love is sweet and colorful! Unfortunately, the female Sheep does not have the same luck. Romantic relationships are unstable and could be ruined by a third party. Married Sheep born in the summer months (June, July, August) have danger signs for getting involved in scandalous affairs.

Your Benefactor is: Tiger
(1926, 1938, 1950, 1962, 1974, 1986, 1998, 2010)

12 Month Outlook For The Sheep

Solar Month	Comments
1st Month Feb 4th - Mar 5th	Sunny skies, life moves upward! Good time for a fresh start or new plans.
2nd Month Mar 6th - Apr 4th	Luck is low. Stress will be higher than usual.
3rd Month Apr 5th - May 4th	A month of gossip. It will be easy to get a traffic ticket or a similar minor problem.
4th Month May 5th - Jun 5th	Conflicts easily arise this month. Tense relationships with friends or family.
5th Month Jun 6th - Jul 6th	Be conservative. Advice about risky investment is untrustworthy.
6th Month Jul 7th - Aug 6th	Watch out for your money. Do not trust others or give loans. Everything is topsy-turvy.
7th Month Aug 7th - Sep 7th	Auspicious stars shine above! You may receive some unexpected benefits. Salaried workers can expect a promotion.
8th Month Sep 8th - Oct 7th	Money luck is good. Take care of your physical health.
9th Month Oct 8th - Nov 6th	Beneficial luck for social relationships.
10th Month Nov 7th - Dec 6th	You may feel unwell or moody frequently.
11th Month Dec 7th - Jan 5th	Good time to develop something new in your life.
12th Month Jan 6th - Feb 3rd	Money and career luck are looking good. A good opportunity comes your way.

The Monkey

Note: The New Year begins February 4th

This year the Monkey has good money luck and career opportunities far from his/her birthplace; if you work hard, you will be rewarded. But local money luck and career (around the birthplace) is unstable this year; it is a time of floating and sinking. Where career is concerned, your gains will not be proportional to your efforts. Be patient and tolerant. Take baby steps, as there is no big leap this year. A number of obstacles and setbacks await you in late spring and early summer. However, luck improves in the second half of the year. Reserve your energy and be well-prepared for a more auspicious time when better opportunities arrive. As for money luck, do not have too many lofty dreams or take short-cuts with risky investments. Some unexpected consuming cannot be avoided. This is not a good year for lending money, even to friends or relatives, as it could ruin your relationships. In health, the Monkey should try to avoid too much tension and stress, as it will be easy to become sick this year. The elderly in your family need to be especially careful, as the Monkey may be in mourning this year. In love, follow the stream - if it comes, it comes. Do not pursue it or have overly high expectations. Married Monkeys must not touch the Peach Blossoms (outside love)! This will lead to separation.

Your Benefactor is: Rabbit
(1927, 1939, 1951, 1963, 1975, 1987, 1999, 2011)

12 Month Outlook For The Monkey

Solar Month	Comments
1st Month Feb 4th - Mar 5th	You may fall sick easily. Refrain from visiting the sick or attending funerals.
2nd Month Mar 6th - Apr 4th	A rather auspicious month. Your career will be smooth sailing.
3rd Month Apr 5th - May 4th	Luck is moving upward. A benefactor may show up, but prevent unnecessary overspending.
4th Month May 5th - Jun 5th	Average luck. Some unexpected consuming cannot be avoided.
5th Month Jun 6th - Jul 6th	It is easy to experience conflict and disharmony. Be less social and stay away from gossip.
6th Month Jul 7th - Aug 6th	Luck is strong. Smooth sailing! A good surprise will come.
7th Month Aug 7th - Sep 7th	Pay attention to your health in order to avoid minor illness.
8th Month Sep 8th - Oct 7th	Steady and smooth sailing. There are good opportunities. Watch out for sharp objects which may cause bleeding.
9th Month Oct 8th - Nov 6th	This is a bumpy month; be conservative in money matters.
10th Month Nov 7th - Dec 6th	Though there is pressure in your life, money and career are looking good.
11th Month Dec 7th - Jan 5th	Life is quite busy socially. Things are pleasurable. Money luck is strong.
12th Month Jan 6th - Feb 3rd	Auspicious luck. Nearly all matters turn out well.

The Rooster

1921, 1933, 1945, 1957, 1969, 1981, 1993, 2005

Note: The New Year begins February 4th

This year brings celebration qi for the Rooster! It will be a happy year. The auspicious Hong Luan and Tai Yin Stars shine above - you may get married, have a baby, receive a promotion, or have another such celebration, one after the other! This energy is especially strong for the female Rooster. For single Roosters, there is a very good chance of a marriage proposal. However, career and money luck are average. In business dealings, the Rooster should put in more time and hard work. Take careful note of all that is going on around, as well as keeping aware of the views of others. It is easy to get into tangles. Pay more attention to your relationships with people. As for money prospects, you are likely to chalk up unnecessary expenditures during autumn, so try to budget wisely. In health, there are no serious problems, but watch your step to prevent accidents; be careful of twisting your ankle or other leg problems. Love is sparkling this year - like a fish in water. Especially in early March and late August, it will be a very auspicious time to offer or receive a marriage proposal. This is a good year for courting couples to get married. Those who are single may meet their ideal life partner. Females born in 1969 and 1981 should avoid getting into a love triangle. Males born in March 1957 should watch for signs of their wife's infidelity.

Your Benefactor is: Snake
(1929, 1941, 1953, 1965, 1977, 1989, 2001, 2013)

12 Month Outlook For The Rooster

Solar Month	Comments
1st Month Feb 4th - Mar 5th	Bathe in the spring breeze! Everything is good and enjoyable. This is a super auspicious time for singles to get married.
2nd Month Mar 6th - Apr 4th	Average luck. You are busy physically and mentally.
3rd Month Apr 5th - May 4th	Luck is low. Keep your emotions under tight control in all situations.
4th Month May 5th - Jun 5th	Be alert for signs of over-spending. Watch out for cash-flow problems and budget wisely.
5th Month Jun 6th - Jul 6th	Good luck. Plot future plans with care; the benefits will be everything you could hope for.
6th Month Jul 7th - Aug 6th	Be cautious; family members could have health problems. Avoid visiting hospitals.
7th Month Aug 7th - Sep 7th	Luck is really good for romance, like an enjoyable spring wind blowing over the land.
8th Month Sep 8th - Oct 7th	Luck is mixed between good and bad. Beware of gossip and backstabbing. Do what you usually do. Say less.
9th Month Oct 8th - Nov 6th	Average luck. You are busy marching forward.
10th Month Nov 7th - Dec 6th	Do all that you can to boost business prospects. Things will come out well.
11th Month Dec 7th - Jan 5th	An unexpected benefactor may come forward. Accept offers without reservation.
12th Month Jan 6th - Feb 3rd	Be conservative. Avoid being hasty or greedy so as to prevent financial mishaps.

The Dog

Note: The New Year begins February 4th

This is a mixed year for the Dog. If you prepare for any contingency, you can go through the year without any mishaps. There are opportunities for you - grab them and work hard. The Horse year is particularly good for young dogs born in 1982. The more you work, the more you gain. The only problem for the Dog is that it is easy to find yourself around "petty people" - backstabbers who may slow down your efforts. The self-employed should act within the confines of their own abilities. Try to do everything yourself and be humble at all time to prevent nasty situations. Salaried workers face lot of pressure, but as long as you work hard, promotions and pay raises are easily yours. Money luck is average; the rewards come only from the efforts you put forth in your work and not as a result of a windfall. Therefore, you should avoid gambling or risky short-cut investments. In health, because money prospects and career are mixed between good and bad, tension and stress are difficult to avoid. Common complaints this year are insomnia and mental stress. Don't work too hard, especially during November. Take care of yourself - money is not everything. In romance, the Dog may have many opportunities for passionate flings but not for long-lasting relationships. Married Dogs need to be more communicative with their partners.

Your Benefactor is: Ox
(1925, 1937, 1949, 1961, 1973, 1985, 1997, 2009)

12 Month Outlook For The Dog

Solar Month	Comments
1st Month Feb 4th - Mar 5th	Things are average to good, but it will be easy to arouse gossip and misunderstandings.
2nd Month Mar 6th - Apr 4th	Be alert of signs of overspending or money loss.
3rd Month Apr 5th - May 4th	Keep on high alert. Big consuming! Spending must cut back to necessities only. Be careful of being cheated.
4th Month May 5th - Jun 5th	Strong luck in career. Try hard to fight for what you want.
5th Month Jun 6th - Jul 6th	Be conservative. Signs of conflict.
6th Month Jul 7th - Aug 6th	Good luck. Plot future plans with care; the benefits will be everything you could hope for.
7th Month Aug 7th - Sep 7th	This is a bumpy month. Do not be aggressive. Be conservative and go step by step.
8th Month Sep 8th - Oct 7th	Normal luck. A new opportunity awaits you.
9th Month Oct 8th - Nov 6th	An unexpected benefactor may come forward. Accept offers without reservation.
10th Month Nov 7th - Dec 6th	Good timing! You will be in the right place at the right time.
11th Month Dec 7th - Jan 5th	Guard against becoming too complacent and overlooking an important matter.
12th Month Jan 6th - Feb 3rd	Conditions stimulate you to try something different.

The Pig

Note: The New Year begins February 4th

In 2014, the Pig's luck is different from 2013 - now your luck is slowly moving forward! This is a moderate year. The Pig must persist in taking the initiative and be decisive in order to gain during the Horse year. Otherwise, things will go downhill. In the first part of the year, you may be busy physically and mentally. Relaxation is your top priority, so put aside all thought of work responsibilities. Luck is low. To be safe, do not visit sick people or attend funerals. The beginning of the second part finds you energetically pursuing a special field of education. This could involve acquiring new skills that further your career. It is an unusually important time. Focus on what is most important first. Stick with it until you are satisfied with results. Great progress can be made this year. Salaried workers have more luck than the self-employed. Money prospects are slow during the spring. Come summer, there is a small consuming star present, so you need to budget wisely. In autumn, pleasant working relationships make this a good season to launch something new. This will facilitate your career development in winter. In health, be careful of food poisoning or alcohol abuse, and do not visit hospitals or go to funerals. In romance, the Pig attracts beautiful, colorful Peach Blossoms! Yet there is no sign of a permanent commitment.

Your Benefactor is: Rat
(1924, 1936, 1948, 1960, 1972, 1984, 1996, 2008)

12 Month Outlook For The Pig

Solar Month	Comments
1st Month Feb 4th - Mar 5th	You are likely to incur unnecessary expenses. Be on guard to keep spending under control.
2nd Month Mar 6th - Apr 4th	Be on high alert. There are signs of conflict or the potential for suffering financial losses.
3rd Month Apr 5th - May 4th	Energy is low. You can easily become inattentive and moody.
4th Month May 5th - Jun 5th	Auspicious money luck. For salaried-workers, there is a future promotion or pay raise.
5th Month Jun 6th - Jul 6th	Luck is average to good. Life is busy.
6th Month Jul 7th - Aug 6th	If you experience disturbing symptoms, be sure to see a doctor for a physical check up.
7th Month Aug 7th - Sep 7th	Enjoyable! Things are flowing smoothly.
8th Month Sep 8th - Oct 7th	Auspicious star smile on you. Substantial gains can be expected.
9th Month Oct 8th - Nov 6th	An unexpected benefactor may come forward. Conditions are fortunate for your interests.
10th Month Nov 7th - Dec 6th	Avoid excesses of any kind, such as eating, drinking, late night partying, or whatever.
11th Month Dec 7th - Jan 5th	Romantic luck is strong. Things are pleasurable.
12th Month Jan 6th - Feb 3rd	Be conservative. This is quite an uneventful month for both career and money luck.

The Rat

Note: The New Year begins February 4ᵗʰ

The Horse year is in conflict with Rat. There can be a kind of revolution in your life - either from good to bad or bad to good, compared to the previous year. Overall, this year's luck indicates that you should not be overly optimistic. Do things "with two hands ready," meaning think twice before taking action. Reign in your emotions under all circumstances. In career luck, things change a lot and are difficult to control. Your gain is not proportional to the great effort you put in, but you will see benefit in the future! Therefore, work hard and don't bargain for immediate benefits. If you are prepared for any contingency, you will go through the year without mishap. In money prospects, you are likely to incur unnecessary expenses. Be on guard; keep expenses under control in February. However, financial losses can be prevented with careful judgment. Avoid gossip and do what you can to avoid break-ins when you take a long leave from your home. Don't do anything risky; otherwise you could get into legal trouble. Health is average good for the Rat this year - stress and insomnia are two problems you should watch for. Where romance is concerned, disputes with your loved one will occur frequently. This is especially true with married couples. Try to be more understanding towards each other.

Your Benefactor is: Dog
(1922, 1934, 1946, 1958, 1970, 1982, 1994, 2006)

12 Month Outlook For The Rat

Solar Month	Comments
1st Month Feb 4th - Mar 5th	A month of conflict. Put a stop to unnecessary overspending.
2nd Month Mar 6th - Apr 4th	Auspicious stars shine above! Good fortune goes hand in hand with you and puts you in the right time, right place.
3rd Month Apr 5th - May 4th	Exercise more and stay away from places such as hospitals where contagious diseases occur.
4th Month May 5th - Jun 5th	Luck is good. The gains will be rather significant from money you invest.
5th Month Jun 6th - Jul 6th	Luck is mixed. Do not be rushed into a decision that will have far-reaching effects.
6th Month Jul 7th - Aug 6th	Taking a business trip or vacation may produce unexpected rewards.
7th Month Aug 7th - Sep 7th	A rewarding month. Most things are to your satisfaction.
8th Month Sep 8th - Oct 7th	A new opportunity awaits you. Beneficial to travel.
9th Month Oct 8th - Nov 6th	Pay attention to your health to prevent illness.
10th Month Nov 7th - Dec 6th	Do all that you can to boost business prospects. Things will come out well.
11th Month Dec 7th - Jan 5th	Things emerge well. Put more effort into reaching your target. Bountiful gains can be expected.
12th Month Jan 6th - Feb 3rd	Be alert for signs of overspending and money loss.

The Ox

Note: The New Year begins February 4th

The Ox finds the Horse a rather auspicious year. Career is given a great boost. After you work hard and insist on what you've planned, you achieve your goals. If you are thinking of changing jobs or expanding your business, beginning in the spring or early summer are the best times to do it. You will get invaluable help from others during autumn. Though this is a relatively good year for the Ox, care must be taken to prevent acts of sabotage arising from jealousy. Money luck is quite strong. This year brings good opportunities for the Ox to make some long-term investments; you will be rewarded abundantly in the future. You may also discover a new source of income. Yet, luck fluctuates for Oxen born in 1973. Don't be greedy or hold high expectations about money beyond your ability. Be calm and don't make decisions when you feel emotional. Health is average. Be careful with outdoor activities. Pay attention when driving, especially during September and October. Where love is concerned, a fruitful romance comes your way. Your relationship with a loved one will progress faster than expected. Spring and summer are ideal times to get married. Married Oxen should be loyal to their loved one - don't attempt to pick wild flowers on the roadside, otherwise there will be regrets.

Your Benefactor is: Dragon
(1928, 1940, 1952, 1964, 1976, 1988, 2000, 2012)

12 Month Outlook For The Ox

Solar Month	Comments
1st Month Feb 4th - Mar 5th	Auspicious stars shine above! Money and career luck are looking good. A good time to offer or receive a marriage proposal!
2nd Month Mar 6th - Apr 4th	Things emerge well. Romantic encounters are plenty. Life is so enjoyable!
3rd Month Apr 5th - May 4th	Luck is smooth sailing. Things go mostly as you wish.
4th Month May 5th - Jun 5th	Double check details that others have turned over to you; their thoroughness is doubtful.
5th Month Jun 6th - Jul 6th	Be conservative. Luck is low. Not beneficial to go out late at night.
6th Month Jul 7th - Aug 6th	Luck is average. Watch out for the flu or getting cut.
7th Month Aug 7th - Sep 7th	This is a relatively favorable month for travel. A sign of strong peach blossom.
8th Month Sep 8th - Oct 7th	Energy is low. You can easily become inattentive and moody.
9th Month Oct 8th - Nov 6th	This month is blessed There are opportunities awaiting at the front door.
10th Month Nov 7th - Dec 6th	Good in money luck. A pay raise may come to salaried workers.
11th Month Dec 7th - Jan 5th	This is a relatively uneasy month: moody and lonely.
12th Month Jan 6th - Feb 3rd	Tense relationships with people. Conflicts easily arise.

The Tiger

Note: The New Year begins February 4ᵗʰ

Generally speaking, this is basically a stable year for the Tiger. Help comes from an unexpected source and a profitable investment opportunity comes your way. Yet this does not mean that you can do whatever you want. You must take advantage of the opportunity by marching steadily forward step by step for anything to be achieved. Salaried workers face pressure, but as long as you work hard, promotion and pay raise are easily yours. After spring, your career or investments may hit a snag. Avoid lending money to or acting as a guarantor for others. It is easy to get involved with backstabbers and gossip, and disharmony with friends is easily aroused. You have to control yourself this year! Although business and money luck are equally strong, you have to handle a lot of tangling obstacles. Work hard, insistently and constantly - your planning is the key to success. Health is generally good, but be cautious with alcohol and sex. Take care of the elderly in your family; older family members (60+) could have health problems. Those born in 1962 should refrain from visiting the sick or attending funerals. In love, the Tiger finds this is a relatively uneventful year for romance - don't expect too much. Married couples should refrain from quarreling; tolerance is the keyword.

Your Benefactor is: Pig
(1923, 1935, 1947, 1959, 1971, 1983, 1995, 2007)

12 Month Outlook For The Tiger

Solar Month	Comments
1st Month Feb 4th - Mar 5th	Good in money luck. Things are satisfying.
2nd Month Mar 6th - Apr 4th	Enjoyable peach blossom; your mate or date knows just how to keep you smiling.
3rd Month Apr 5th - May 4th	Double-check details that others have turned over to you; their thoroughness is doubtful.
4th Month May 5th - Jun 5th	Taking a business or vacation trip may produce unexpected rewards.
5th Month Jun 6th - Jul 6th	A good time to develop something new.
6th Month Jul 7th - Aug 6th	A benefactor star shines above, an unexpected good surprise will come.
7th Month Aug 7th - Sep 7th	A month filled with depression and frustration. Restrain yourself from any type of argument or fight.
8th Month Sep 8th - Oct 7th	For femles, career and love are both happy, but they are frustrating for males.
9th Month Oct 8th - Nov 6th	Say less and be humble. There are signs that gossip will tangle things up.
10th Month Nov 7th - Dec 6th	Refrain from visiting the sick or attending funerals.
11th Month Dec 7th - Jan 5th	Career luck is smooth. Look out for signs of overspending or financial loss.
12th Month Jan 6th - Feb 3rd	Sunny skies! Lots of social opportunities. There are signs of an unexpected benefactor showing up.

The Rabbit

Note: The New Year begins February 4ᵗʰ

This is a relatively good year for the Rabbit with good career and money prospects.

It is also a good time to venture beyond your usual scope. If you are thinking of changing jobs or striking out on your own, this is the best time to do so. If you plan it well you will receive an amazing reward! The self-employed will have more opportunities for further development than salaried workers. A career switch will bring good results. This year, if you intend to go into a partnership, it is best to approach people born in the Sheep or Ox year. Money luck is moving up steadily. Even though there is some spending, you still receive much more back. This is a good year for investments and there is no harm in buying a lottery ticket to try your auspicious luck during this Horse year. In health, it is easy to have some sort of bleeding problem. Injuries to your limbs and head may result from accidents. A frightening experience awaits you if you travel in autumn, so pay more attention in order to avoid traffic accidents, cuts, and burns. Be especially careful outdoors late at night. This is quite an uneven year for romance. One moment, you and you partner are at your most loving; the next, you behave like mortal enemies. Married couples should refrain from quarreling; otherwise, you both have a lot to lose.

Your Benefactor is: Rooster
(1933, 1945, 1957, 1969, 1981, 1993, 2005)

12 Month Outlook For The Rabbit

Solar Month	Comments
1st Month Feb 4th - Mar 5th	This is a rewarding month for both romance and business.
2nd Month Mar 6th - Apr 4th	All things are relatively peaceful.
3rd Month Apr 5th - May 4th	A career or job switch brings favorable results.
4th Month May 5th - Jun 5th	Beneficial luck for social relationships.
5th Month Jun 6th - Jul 6th	Money prospects are at their best for males; life is average for females.
6th Month Jul 7th - Aug 6th	Be conservative. It is not a suitable time to make important decisions.
7th Month Aug 7th - Sep 7th	Stay on high alert. A sign of relationship breakup or cuts.
8th Month Sep 8th - Oct 7th	Average luck in domestic affairs. Exceptionally good for venturing overseas.
9th Month Oct 8th - Nov 6th	Beware of falling into a trap. For males stay away from alcohol and sex.
10th Month Nov 7th - Dec 6th	Do not trust anyone blindly lest you get cheated.
11th Month Dec 7th - Jan 5th	This month holds good fortune for proceeding with something new or expanding your career.
12th Month Jan 6th - Feb 3rd	Luck is neither auspicious nor inauspicious

The Dragon

1928, 1940, 1952, 1964, 1976, 1988, 2000, 2012

Note: The New Year begins February 4ᵗʰ

Even though 2014 is not so smooth, the Dragon does have some auspicious stars to help. Eventually things improve - you can break through difficulties and achieve your goals. In career, there is some conflict and fighting. Remember, if you are humble and make concessions, things will be softened. Be wary of a trusted assistant or friend turning against you in June or December. Your favorable months are May and November. Expand your social circle and take the initiative to improve interpersonal relationships. This facilitates your development for next year. Money luck is not bad, but it is easy come, easy go. It is not easy to keep balance. Try not to get involved in gossip circles. Employees may receive a promotion this year! The Dragon is busy and has a lot of activities. Money luck is not good for risky investments or gambling. In health, watch out for your digestive system and joints may give you problems. Those born in 1952 should take special notice. This is quite an uneven year for romance. You are very emotional, easily aroused to argue and lose control of yourself; one moment, you and your partner are at your most loving, the next, you behave like mortal enemies. The best way to avoid this is to be patient and don't nitpick or argue. Married couples should refrain from quarreling; otherwise, you both have a lot to lose.

Your Benefactor is: Sheep
(1919, 1931, 1943, 1955, 1967, 1979, 1991, 2003)

12 Month Outlook For The Dragon

Solar Month	Comments
1st Month Feb 4th - Mar 5th	Luck is neither auspicious nor inauspicious.
2nd Month Mar 6th - Apr 4th	It is an auspicious time to study or to learn something new.
3rd Month Apr 5th - May 4th	Powerful sign of luck. Hard work will achieve favorable results.
4th Month May 5th - Jun 5th	Luck and harmony are in sync. You see much hope and many opportunities.
5th Month Jun 6th - Jul 6th	Be conservative. Signs of conflict.
6th Month Jul 7th - Aug 6th	Luck is steadily going up and career and money prospects are good.
7th Month Aug 7th - Sep 7th	Be satisfied with small gains; do not expect too much.
8th Month Sep 8th - Oct 7th	This is a month of conflict and tension. Keep plans low-key and take a relaxing travel.
9th Month Oct 8th - Nov 6th	Cast aside any thoughts of greed if you want to prevent financial mishaps.
10th Month Nov 7th - Dec 6th	Good aspects are seen in almost everything. Long distance business ventures are promising.
11th Month Dec 7th - Jan 5th	Relaxation is the top priority this month. Put aside all thought of work responsibilities.
12th Month Jan 6th - Feb 3rd	Pleasant working relationships make this a good month to launch a new project.

The Snake

Note: The New Year begins February 4ᵗʰ

With the Wen Chang star in your Ming Palace, this is a significant year in education for the Snake. There are some important work projects and exams, as well as the chance to choose a subject to specialize in. The best time for you to proceed with your ambition is in the late spring and summer.

Money prospects are average and steadily coming in. However, do not gamble or make risky investments. Money will be consumed and there is no need to argue about what you must spend. With an inauspicious star named Guan Fu shining above, be careful in business with others and don't be greedy for immediate benefit. Do not use underhanded ways or take short cuts to make money; it may get you into trouble with the law. Those born between the 29th of April and the 28th of May should be extra careful of getting into trouble with the law over documents you sign. Whether male or female, it is easy to be involved with gossip and entanglements. Pay attention to your health - caution is the watchword of the year. If you feel at all uncomfortable, go to the doctor right away! Avoid going to funerals or visiting someone in the hospital. Romance is very sensitive and complicated. You will find it quite difficult to discern love and hate. Try not to be too sensitive so that you avoid unnecessary misunderstandings. Married Snakes find it especially easy to have misunderstandings and miscommunication.

Your Benefactor is: Monkey
(1920, 1932, 1944, 1956, 1968, 1980, 1992, 2004)

12 Month Outlook For The Snake

Solar Month	Comments
1st Month Feb 4th - Mar 5th	Inauspicious luck is foreseen in money matters. You are likely to incur unnecessary expenditures.
2nd Month Mar 6th - Apr 4th	Auspicious stars shine above! Good aspects are seen in almost everything.
3rd Month Apr 5th - May 4th	Luck is noticeably moving upward. Matters turn out well in nearly all aspects.
4th Month May 5th - Jun 5th	Things are uncertain. A 'wait and see' attitude is the best policy.
5th Month Jun 6th - Jul 6th	Conditions are easygoing and comfortable.
6th Month Jul 7th - Aug 6th	Keep all moves simple and straightforward so that no one can accuse you of deception.
7th Month Aug 7th - Sep 7th	Guard against illness, maybe the flu.
8th Month Sep 8th - Oct 7th	Watch out for signs of overspending or money loss.
9th Month Oct 8th - Nov 6th	Strong good luck. Put more effort into hitting your target. The gains are bountiful.
10th Month Nov 7th - Dec 6th	Tense relationships with people. Conflicts easily arise.
11th Month Dec 7th - Jan 5th	Things are pleasurable! Enjoy the happy mood.
12th Month Jan 6th - Feb 3rd	Be conservative; this month is quite uncertain. It is beneficial to travel and have the sun shine on you.

There is no secret to success,
but hard work

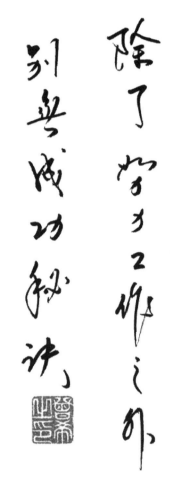

Calligraphy by Larry Sang

LI MING

TABLE 1

LI MING (establish fate): STEP 1: DETERMINE YOUR PALACE

LI MING for 2014

立 命 立 命

This is another system for making annual predictions:

★ First, use Table 1, based on your month and time of birth.
★ Take the results of Table 1, and use them in Table 2, along with your year of birth, to find the palace of Li Ming for 2014.
★ Once you know the palace of Li Ming, read the prediction that follows for that palace.

Birth Hour:		Born After:											
		Jan 21 1st Month	Feb 19 2nd Month	Mar 20 3rd Month	Apr 20 4th Month	May 21 5th Month	Jun 21 6th Month	Jul 23 7th Month	Aug 23 8th Month	Sep 23 9th Month	Oct 23 10th Month	Nov 22 11th Month	Dec 22 12th Month
Zi	11pm-1am	Mao	Yin	Chou	Zi	Hai	Xu	You	Shen	Wei	Wu	Si	Chen
Chou	1-3am	Yin	Chou	Zi	Hai	Xu	You	Shen	Wei	Wu	Si	Chen	Mao
Yin	3-5am	Chou	Zi	Hai	Xu	You	Shen	Wei	Wu	Si	Chen	Mao	Yin
Mao	5-7am	Zi	Hai	Xu	You	Shen	Wei	Wu	Si	Chen	Mao	Yin	Chou
Chen	7-9am	Hai	Xu	You	Shen	Wei	Wu	Si	Chen	Mao	Yin	Chou	Zi
Si	9-11am	Xu	You	Shen	Wei	Wu	Si	Chen	Mao	Yin	Chou	Zi	Hai
Wu	11am-1pm	You	Shen	Wei	Wu	Si	Chen	Mao	Yin	Chou	Zi	Hai	Xu
Wei	1-3pm	Shen	Wei	Wu	Si	Chen	Mao	Yin	Chou	Zi	Hai	Xu	You
Shen	3-5pm	Wei	Wu	Si	Chen	Mao	Yin	Chou	Zi	Hai	Xu	You	Shen
You	5-7pm	Wu	Si	Chen	Mao	Yin	Chou	Zi	Hai	Xu	You	Shen	Wei
Xu	7-9pm	Si	Chen	Mao	Yin	Chou	Zi	Hai	Xu	You	Shen	Wei	Wu
Hai	9-11pm	Chen	Mao	Yin	Chou	Zi	Hai	Xu	You	Shen	Wei	Wu	Si

Notes:

These months are different from the solar (Feng Shui/Four Pillars) months, and also are different from the lunar months. They begin on the *Qi* of the *Twenty-Four Jieqi*. If born within a day of these month dates, please consult a *Ten-Thousand Year Calendar* to determine exactly which is your birth month in this system. It is not necessary for you to understand the Chinese terms in the tables. Just follow the tables to the correct palace for you.

TABLE 2

立命 LI MING (establish fate): STEP 2: PALACE FOR A WU (HORSE) YEAR 立命 LI MING for 2014

Li Ming:	Birth Year:											
	Rat Zi	Ox Chou	Tiger Yin	Rabbit Mao	Dragon Chen	Snake Si	Horse Wu	Sheep Wei	Monkey Shen	Rooster You	Dog Xu	Pig Hai
Zi	Wu	Wei	Shen	You	Xu	Hai	Zi	Chou	Yin	Mao	Chen	Si
Chou	Wei	Shen	You	Xu	Hai	Zi	Chou	Yin	Mao	Chen	Si	Wu
Yin	Shen	You	Xu	Hai	Zi	Chou	Yin	Mao	Chen	Si	Wu	Wei
Mao	You	Xu	Hai	Zi	Chou	Yin	Mao	Chen	Si	Wu	Wei	Shen
Chen	Xu	Hai	Zi	Chou	Yin	Mao	Chen	Si	Wu	Wei	Shen	You
Si	Hai	Zi	Chou	Yin	Mao	Chen	Si	Wu	Wei	Shen	You	Xu
Wu	Zi	Chou	Yin	Mao	Chen	Si	Wu	Wei	Shen	You	Xu	Hai
Wei	Chou	Yin	Mao	Chen	Si	Wu	Wei	Shen	You	Xu	Hai	Zi
Shen	Yin	Mao	Chen	Si	Wu	Wei	Shen	You	Xu	Hai	Zi	Chou
You	Mao	Chen	Si	Wu	Wei	Shen	You	Xu	Hai	Zi	Chou	Yin
Xu	Chen	Si	Wu	Wei	Shen	You	Xu	Hai	Zi	Chou	Yin	Mao
Hai	Si	Wu	Wei	Shen	You	Xu	Hai	Zi	Chou	Yin	Mao	Chen

Notes:

★ Take the Palace of Li Ming, found in Table 1, and compare it to the year of birth to find the palace for 2014, a Wu (Horse) year.

★ Use January 21st as the beginning of the new year for finding the birth year. If the date falls within one day of January 21st, check in a *Ten-Thousand Year Calendar* to be sure. If the birth date is between January 1st and January 20th, consider the person as belonging to the previous year in this system.

★ The predictions described below go from January 20th, 2014 until January 19th, 2015.

LI MING PALACE READING

Zi

Your Li Ming contains Da Hao and Sui Po, so there may be some kind of revolution in your life. It is a challenging and unstable year; you should not be overly optimistic. There is the possibility of financial mishaps related to business contracts or taking place within the family. Do not expect windfalls; avoid gambling or indulging in financial speculation. Be extra careful around all kinds of vehicles while traveling; drive defensively and be sure to use your seat belt. Plenty of rest is needed to overcome mental exhaustion.

Chou

This is a rather auspicious year. Career is given a great boost if you work hard and insist on what you've planned. You will get invaluable help from others. Money luck is quite strong. There are good opportunities for making some long-term investments that will have abundant rewards in the future. But don't be greedy or hold high expectations about money beyond your abilities. Be calm and don't make decisions when you feel emotional. Be careful in outdoor activities. Pay attention while driving. A fruitful romance comes your way.

Yin

This is a stable year. Help comes from an unexpected source and a profitable investment opportunity comes your way. Salaried workers face pressure, but as long as you work hard, promotion and pay raise are easily yours. You have to handle a lot of tangling obstacles. Avoid lending money to people or acting as a guarantor for others. It is easy to become involved with backstabbers and gossip, and disharmony with friends is easily aroused. Take care of the elderly in your family; older family members (60+) could have health problems.

Mao

This is a relatively good year for career and money prospects. If you are thinking of changing jobs, this is the best time to do so; if you plan it well you receive an amazing reward! The self-employed have more opportunity for further development than salaried workers. A career switch brings good results. Money luck moves up steadily. In health, it is easy to have some sort of bleeding. Injuries to your limbs and head may result from accidents. Pay more attention to avoid traffic accidents; be especially careful outdoors late at night.

Chen

If Li Ming is here, it is not so smooth; yet there are some auspicious stars to help you. Eventually things become better - you can break through the difficulties and achieve your goals. In career, there are some conflicts and fighting. If you are humble and make concessions, things will be softened. Expand your social circle and take the initiative to improve interpersonal relationships. Money luck is not bad, but it is easy come, easy go. Try not to get involved in gossip circles. This is not a good year for romance because there are frequent squabbles.

Si

With the Wen Chang star here, this is a significant year for education and exam-taking, as well as for choosing a subject to specialize in. Money prospects are average but it comes in steadily. With an inauspicious star named Guan Fu shining above, be careful in business with others and don't be greedy for immediate benefits. Do not use underhanded ways or take short cuts to make money; this may get you into trouble with the law. It is easy to have gossip and entanglements. Avoid going to funerals or visiting hospitals. Pay attention to your health - caution is the watchword of the year.

Wu

With a brilliant money star shining above, money luck is extremely strong. 2014 is a particularly rewarding year. Although you meet with a lot of pressure and competition in your work, luck is on your side. But guard against greed; don't push your luck with risky investments. Career and money prospects are at their best during the summer and early autumn. Salaried workers may discover a new source of income, and lucrative opportunities should present themselves. Be careful of falling from high places and of travel accidents.

Wei

With Li Ming here, males can take a big step forward in career. The wind is at your back. Whatever you want will come easily to you. Grab the opportunity and work hard. Good money prospects enable your saving to grow, due to an auspicious star shining above. However, it is a mixed fortune for females. Do not rush or act irrationally; otherwise it is likely that you encounter difficulties and danger. Avoid gambling or financial speculation. Try to refrain from overworking lest you be stricken by illness.

Shen

There are good opportunities for someone who goes far from his or her birthplace for money luck and career; hard work is rewarded. But money luck and career locally (at the birthplace) are unstable this year; it is a time of floating and sinking. A number of obstacles and setbacks await you. Do not have too many lofty dreams or take short-cuts with risky investments. Some unexpected consuming cannot be avoided. This is not a good year for lending money to friends or relatives. The elderly in your family need to be especially careful; there is a sign of the possibility of wearing mourning clothes. Avoid visiting the sick and attending funerals.

You

If your Li Ming here, this will be a happy year. The auspicious Hong Luan and Tai Yin stars shine above - you may get married, have a baby, receive a promotion, or have other such celebrations, coming one after another! This energy is especially strong for females. For single people, there is a very good chance of a marriage proposal. However, career and money luck are average. In business dealings, it is easy to get tangled up. Pay more attention to your relationships. Love is sparkling; this is a good year for courting couples to get married.

Xu

This is a mixed year. Be prepared for any contingency and you will go through the year without mishaps. There are opportunities - grab them and work hard. The more you work, the more you gain. The self-employed should act within the confines of their own abilities. Try to do everything yourself and be humble at all times to prevent nasty situations. Salaried workers face a lot of pressure, but as long as you work hard, promotion and pay raise are easily yours. Money luck is average; the rewards will come only from the efforts you put forth in your work and not as the result of a windfall.

Hai

This is a moderate year. Things are relatively peaceful. You may feel busy physically and mentally. Relaxation is the top priority, so put aside all thought of work responsibilities. To be safe, do not visit sick people or attend funerals. Great progress can be made if you energetically pursue a special field of education. This could involve acquiring new skills that will further your career. Salaried workers have more luck than the self-employed. There is a small consuming star present, so you need to budget wisely.

LIU REN

LIU REN (六壬)(小六壬)

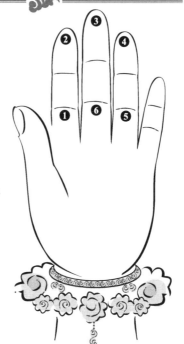

1. Great Peace
2. Back & Forth
3. Hastening Happiness
4. Red Mouth
5. Small Auspiciousness
6. Empty & Lost

Calculation:

When something out of the ordinary spontaneously happens, you can determine the meaning of the omen with *Liu Ren*.

Here is the calculation:

1. Use the left hand. Start in position 1, Great Peace (大安 da an) and always move clockwise.
2. Count clockwise through the six positions for today's *lunar* month. The Great Peace position corresponds to the first lunar month. (Refer to *Ten-Thousand Year Calendar* page at the end of this *Guide*. Find today's date, then read the month number at the top of the column).
3. Count the position found in Step 2 as the first day of the lunar month. Count clockwise through the six positions to today, the current day of the lunar month. (Find today's date in the *Ten-Thousand Year Calendar* page, then read the day number on the side at the end of the row).

4. Count the position found in Step 3 as the first double hour. Count clockwise through the six positions to the current double hour.
5. Look up the interpretation of this palace on page 44 - 45.

Hour Table

Hour	During Standard Time	During Daylight Savings Time
1	11 pm - 1 am	midnight to 2 am
2	1 - 3 am	2 - 4 am
3	3 - 5 am	4 - 6 am
4	5 - 7 am	6 - 8 am
5	7 - 9 am	8 - 10 am
6	9 - 11 am	10 - noon
7	11 am - 1 pm	noon to 2 pm
8	1 - 3 pm	2 - 4 pm
9	3 - 5 pm	4 - 6 pm
10	5 - 7 pm	6 - 8 pm
11	7 - 9 pm	8 - 10 pm
12	9 - 11 pm	10 - midnight

Note: for 11 pm to midnight during standard time, use the next day's date. For example, if it is 11:15 pm on February 12th, then count it as February 13th.

Example: August 6th, 2014, 8:30 am

A. Start in Position One.
B. August 6th is in the column that says 7th month at the top. So we go to Position One.
C. August 6th is the 11th day of the 7th month.
D. Start where we left off in Position One and call that 1. Count clockwise to the 11th position from there: Position Three.
E. Start in Position Three and count for the hour.
F. Whether it is Daylight Savings Time or not, 8:30 am is the 5th hour. Count 5 positions, with Position Three and call that 1, and end up in Position One.

This is the outcome:

Position Five is **Great Peace**
Read the interpretation on the next page and apply it to the situation.

Interpretation

1. Great Peace (大安 da an):

The person in question has not moved at this time. This position belongs to wood element and the east. Generally in planning matters, use 1, 5, and 7. This position belongs to the four limbs. Helpful people are found in the southwest. Avoid the east. Children, women and the six domestic animals are frightened.

In Great Peace, every activity prospers. Seek wealth in the southwest. Lost items are not far away. The house is secure and peaceful. The person you expect has not left yet. Illness is not serious. Military generals return home to the fields. Look for opportunities and push your luck.

2. Back and Forth (留連 liu lian):

The person you expect is not returning yet. This position belongs to water element and the north. Generally in planning matters, use 2, 8, and 10. This position belongs to the kidneys and stomach. Helpful people are found in the south. Avoid the north. Children wander the road as disembodied spirits.

With Back and Forth, activities are difficult to achieve. You have not adequately planned for your goals. Official activities are delayed. Those who have gone do not return from their journey yet. Lost items appear in the south. Hurry and ask for what you want and you will get results. But guard against gossip and disputes. Family members for the moment are so-so.

3. Hastening Happiness (速喜 su xi):

The expected person arrives shortly. This position belongs to fire element and the south. Generally in planning matters, use 3, 6, and 9. This position belongs to the heart and brain. Helpful people are found in the southwest. Avoid the south. Children, women, and animals are frightened.

With Hastening Happiness, happiness arrives. Seek wealth toward the south. Lost items are found between 11 am and 5 pm if you ask a passerby about it. Official activities have blessing and virtue. Sick people have no misfortune. Auspicious for the fields, house, and the six livestock. You receive news from someone far away.

4. Red Mouth (赤口 chi kou)

An inauspicious time for official activities. This position belongs to metal element and the west. Generally in planning matters, use 4, 7, and 10. This position belongs to the lungs and stomach. Helpful people are found in the east. Avoid the west. Children are bewildered young spirits.

Red Mouth governs quarrels and disputes. Be cautious about legal matters. Quickly go search for lost items. Travelers experience a fright. The six domestic animals give you trouble. The sick should go to the west. Furthermore, you must guard against being cursed. Fear catching epidemic diseases.

5. Small Auspiciousness (小吉 xiao ji)

The expected person comes in a happy time. This person belongs to wood element and all directions. Generally in planning matters, use 1, 5, and 7. This position belongs to the liver and intestines. Helpful people are found in the southwest. Avoid the east. Children, women and the six domestic animals are frightened.

Small Auspiciousness is most auspicious and prosperous. Your road is smooth. Spirits come announcing good news. Lost items are located in the southwest. Travelers promptly arrive. Relations with others are extremely strong. Everything is harmonious. A sick person should pray to heaven.

6. Empty and Lost (空亡 kong wang)

News you expect does not come at this time. This position belongs to earth element. Generally in planning matters, use 3, 6, and 9. This position belongs to the spleen and brain. Helpful people are found in the north. Watch out for the health of your children. Males feel pressure. The activities of females get no results.

Spirits are often unreasonable or perverse. Seeking wealth is without benefit. There is disaster for travelers. Lost items will not appear. Official activities bring punishment and damage. Sick people meet a dark ghost. To be secure and peaceful, get release from calamity by sacrifice and prayer.

Example: You are getting married. The limo driver is unable to pick up the bridal party because the tires blew out. You use Liu Ren to find out what is going on.

Today's time and date: March 30th, 2014, 10:30 am

A. Start in Position One.
B. March 30th is in the column that says 2nd month at the top. So we go to Position Two.
   March 30th is the 30th day of the 2nd month.
   Start where we left off in Position Two and call that 1.
C. Count clockwise to the 30th position from there: Position One. Start in Position One and count for the hour.
   It is 10:30 am, the 6th hour.
D. Count 6 positions, with Position One as the beginning, and end up in Position Six.

This is the outcome:

Position Three is **Empty and Lost**
Read the text and apply it to the situation. Empty and Lost begins with "A new limo was sent within." You wait calmly for twenty minutes and your ride arrives. The ride was upgraded to a hummer limo and comped the first 2 hours of service.

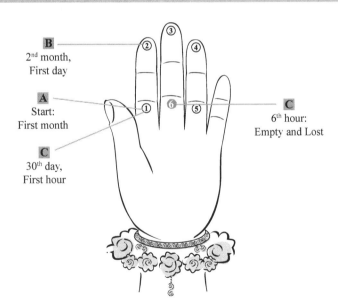

B
2nd month,
First day

A
Start:
First month

C
30th day,
First hour

C
6th hour:
Empty and Lost

OMEN

OMENS

In Chinese almanacs, there are often listings of predictions based on omens. We include a few below. Have fun with it and don't take it seriously.

Omens from the Twitch of an Eye

Time	Eye	This is an omen of:
11 pm - 1 am Zi	Left	Meeting a benefactor
	Right	Having a good meal
1 - 3 am Chou	Left	Having anxiety
	Right	Someone thinking about you
3 - 5 am Yin	Left	Someone coming from afar
	Right	A happy matter arriving
5 - 7 am Mao	Left	The coming of an important guest
	Right	Something peaceful, safe and auspicious
7 - 9 am Chen	Left	A guest coming from afar
	Right	Injury or harm
9 - 11 am Si	Left	Having a good meal
	Right	Something inauspicious
11 am - 1 pm Wu	Left	Having a good meal
	Right	An inauspicious matter
1 - 3 pm Wei	Left	A lucky star
	Right	Good luck, but small
3 - 5 pm Shen	Left	Money coming
	Right	Someone thinking of you romantically
5 - 7 pm You	Left	A guest coming
	Right	A guest arriving
7 - 9 pm Xu	Left	A guest arriving
	Right	A gathering or meeting
9 - 11 pm Hai	Left	A guest arriving
	Right	Gossip

Correct for *Daylight Savings Time*, if in use (subtract one hour from the current time).

Omens from Hiccoughs

Time	This is an omen of:
11 pm - 1 am Zi	A good meal and a happy dinner gathering
1 - 3 am Chou	Someone missing you; a guest coming to seek your help
3 - 5 am Yin	Someone missing you; a dining engagement
5 - 7 am Mao	Wealth and happiness; someone coming to ask about a matter
7 - 9 am Chen	A good meal; great good luck for everyone
9 - 11 am Si	A lucky person coming to seek wealth
11 am - 1 pm Wu	An important guest; someone wanting a dinner gathering
1 - 3 pm Wei	Someone wanting a meal; lucky activities
3 - 5 pm Shen	Nightmares; eating is not beneficial
5 - 7 pm You	Someone coming; someone asks about a matter
7 - 9 pm Xu	Someone missing you; a meeting brings benefit
9 - 11 pm Hai	Something frightens, but on the contrary, brings benefit

Correct for *Daylight Savings Time*, if in use (subtract one hour from the current time).

Man is the artificer
of his own happiness

Calligraphy by Larry Sang

THE YELLOW EMPEROR

THE YELLOW EMPEROR
IN THE FOUR SEASONS

黄帝四季詩

SPRING

AUTUMN

SUMMER

WINTER

There is a lifetime prediction commonly found in Chinese almanacs. Based on your season of birth, find your birth time.

The Yellow Emperor in the Four Seasons

Time of Birth		Season of Birth			
		Spring February 4th to May 4th	**Summer** May 5th to August 6th	**Autumn** August 7th to November 6th	**Winter** November 7th to February 3th
Zi	11p-1a	head	low abdomen	shoulders	low abdomen
Chou	1-3a	chest	hands	hands	knees
Yin	3-5a	feet	feet	knees	chest
Mao	5-7a	shoulders	shoulders	chest	shoulders
Chen	7-9a	knees	knees	feet	feet
Si	9-11a	hands	hands	hands	head
Wu	11a-1p	low abdomen	head	shoulders	hands
Wei	1-3p	hands	chest	chest	knees
Shen	3-5p	feet	feet	low abdomen	chest
You	5-7p	shoulders	shoulders	knees	shoulders
Xu	7-9p	knees	knees	feet	feet
Hai	9-11p	chest	chest	head	hands

Correct birth time for Daylight Saving Time, if used at the time of birth. If you were born in the Southern Hemisphere, switch the autumn and spring dates, as well as the summer and winter dates.

The Yellow Emperor in the Four Seasons

Born on the Yellow Emperor's Head means a lifetime of never having worries. Even petty people have riches and honor. Clothes and food naturally come around. Your position in society is elevated, and gentlemen are good at planning. Women go through life steadily and smoothly, marrying a talented and educated person.

Born on the Yellow Emperor's Hands means business capital is sufficient. Going out, you meet a benefactor. Inside the home, you have everything. Your early years are very steady and smooth. You accumulate many possessions. Wealth comes from every direction. When old, it is in your hands.

The Yellow Emperor in the Four Seasons

Born on the Yellow Emperor's Shoulders means a life of a million riches. You have wealth in your middle years. Children and grandchildren are plenty. Clothes and income at all times are good. In old age, you have fields in the village. Siblings are helpful. Your early life is bitter, but the later end is sweet.

Born on the Yellow Emperor's Chest means clothes and food are naturally ample. Experts in the pen and the sword are around you. There is music, song, and dance. Middle age brings good clothes and food. Later years are happy and prosperous. Joy, utmost honor, prosperity, and increased longevity add more blessings.

Born on the Yellow Emperor's Lower Abdomen, you were treasured by your parents. In middle age, clothes and food are good. When old you obtain gold. The family reputation is changing a lot. You are a noble person. Children and grandchildren must newly shine. Cultured and bright, they advance a lot.

Born on the Yellow Emperor's Knees means doing things is without benefit. In your early years, you toiled a lot, but did not lack clothes and food. Everyday, you travel on the road; you cannot avoid running back and forth. Old age is smooth, with honor and prosperity, but in middle age, hard work is extreme.

Born on the Yellow Emperor's Feet, practice moral teachings to avoid toil. A lifetime that is safe and sound, but unsuitable to reside in your ancestor's home. Women marry two husbands. Men have two wives. Search lonely mountain ranges. Leave your homeland to achieve good fortune.

FENG SHUI

FENG SHUI

Makes the Universe Work for You

 We live in a universe that is filled with different energies. Our planet rotates on its axis, creating cycles of day and night. The earth also revolves around the sun in yearly cycles and is subject to various gravitational and magnetic fields. Our solar system is moving through space and is also subject to other forces in the universe. These physical forces and many different time cycles affects us profoundly. The Chinese have spent centuries observing the effects with their environment. This is the science and art of Feng Shui (Chinese geomancy).

Feng Shui uses observation, repeatable calculations and methodologies, and is based on the study of the environment, both inside and out of the house. Feng Shui can help you determine the best home to live in, which colors can enhance your home, the best bed positions for deep sleep, and how to change your business or home into a center of power. Feng Shui can help improve your health, your relationships and your prosperity. It is based on a complex calculation and observation of the environment, rather than a metaphysical reading relying on inspiration or intuition.

The American Feng Shui Institute publishes the annual Chinese Astrology and Feng Shui Guide so that both the Feng Shui professional and layperson can benefit from the knowledge of the incoming energy cycles and their influences. With this knowledge, one can adjust their environment to make it as harmonious as possible for the current year.

The following sections contain the energy patterns for the current year with an analysis and remedy for each of the eight directions. For the nonprofessional, there is a section on how to prepare your home for this reading. Please note that Feng Shui is a deep and complex science that requires many years to master. Preparing your home to receive the annual energy is one aspect that anyone can apply. A professional reading is recommended to anyone who wishes to receive the greatest benefits possible that Feng Shui can bring.

Preparing your home for a Feng Shui reading

The Floor Plan

The first requirement for preparing your home for a Feng Shui annual reading is to create a proportional floor plan. This plan can be hand drawn or be the original building plans, as long as the plan is proportionally correct. It is not necessary to draw in all your furniture except perhaps noting your bed and desk. It is important that you indicate where all window and door openings are.

Example B
Floor Plan

Example A
Floor Plan

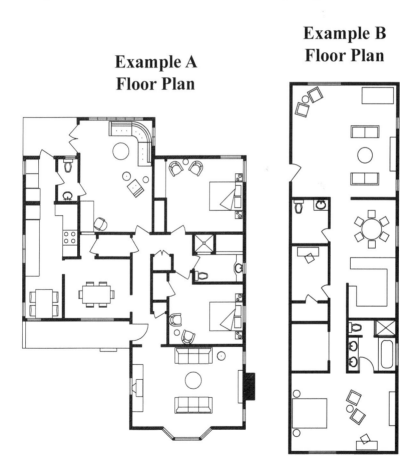

Preparing your home for a Feng Shui reading

Gridding The Floor Plan

Once you have your floor plan drawn, you then overlay a 9 - square grid. This grid is proportional to the floor plan. If it were a long and narrow house, so would the grid be long and narrow. You want to divide the floor plan into equal thirds both top to bottom and left to right as shown below:

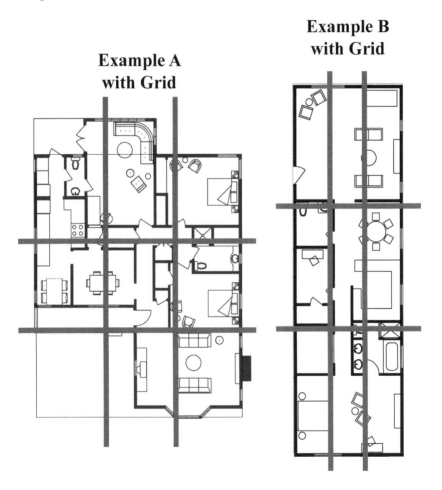

Example B with Grid

Example A with Grid

The Compass Reading

The next step is to determine the alignment of your house with the earth magnetic fields by taking a compass reading. It is very important to take an accurate reading and not guess the orientation based on the direction of the sun or a map.

Why Do You Need To Use A Compass?

In Feng Shui, we look at the eight cardinal and inter-cardinal directions: East, Southeast, South, Southwest, West, Northwest, North, and Northeast when analyzing a home or building. Each of these directions hold unique significance to these building. If you do not use a compass to determine the correct orientation, you might completely misread your home. You cannot map the qi within the building without an exact orientation. It is similar to finding your way out of a forest without a compass. You have a high probability of getting lost. Without a compass, it simply is not Feng Shui.

A Compass vs A Luopan

You can use any compass if you do not have a Luopan. The Luopan is simply a Chinese compass that helps determine the sitting direction of a building. It also contains a wealth of information on its dial that is used for more advanced applications. In recent years, Master Larry Sang simplified the traditional Luopan specifically for training Western students. Although it looks simple compared to an original Luopan, it has all the tools you need to accurately analyze a building. An important fact to remember about a Luopan is that it points to the South. The following information and instructions apply to a Luopan, however, if you are using a Western compass these concepts are easy to adapt.

SANG'S LUOPAN

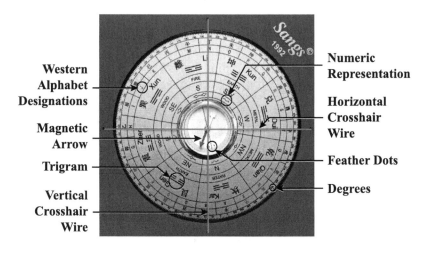

Western Alphabet Designations

Magnetic Arrow

Trigram

Vertical Crosshair Wire

Numeric Representation

Horizontal Crosshair Wire

Feather Dots

Degrees

Parts of Sang's Luopan

The Magnetic Arrow - The arrowhead points South rather than North. Western compasses point North.

The Feather Dots - (The twin dots at the center of the rotating dial). Always adjust the rotating (gold) dial to align the twin dots with the feather end of the arrow.

The Numeric Representations - The innermost ring has a dot pattern that represents the Trigram' numbers. For example Kun has two dots and Qian has six dots.

Crosshair Alignments - The red crosshairs designate the facing and sitting directions. Once the arrow is steady and the feather end is aligned over the north twin dots, you can determine the sitting direction and the facing direction.

The Eight Trigrams - The Eight Trigrams are the basis for orientation in Feng Shui and are shown on the Luopan with their perspective elements, symbols, and directions.

Western Alphabet Designations - Each Trigram is divided into three equal parts. These parts are shown with both their Chinese symbols and using the Western Alphabet.

The Degrees - Outermost on the dial are the Western compass degree in Arabic numerals.

General Guidelines for using the Luopan:

To use the Luopan or compass correctly, remember the following guidelines:

1. Always stand straight and upright.

2. Do not wear metal jewelry or belt buckles that can skew the compass.

3. Avoid any electrical influences such as automobiles or electrical boxes.

4. Always stand parallel to the building.

5. Keep your feet square below you.

6. You can keep the Luopan in the lower box case to manage it better.

Taking a reading with the Luopan:

With the general guidelines for using a luopan in mind, now you ar ready to take a reading to determine which wall or corner of your home is located closest to the North.

1. Take your reading outside, standing parallel to your home with your back to it. Stand straight and hold the Luopan at waist level. Wait until the arrow ceases to quiver.

2. Slowly turn the center (gold) dial so that the North/feather dots aligh with the feather of the arrow. If using a Western compass, turn the compass so that the needle's arrow end aligns with north (between 337.5° - 22.5°).

3. Please take at least three separate readings from other positions. If you find that there is a discrepancy, take various readings at various locations until you are sure which one is correct. One direction should stand out as being correct.

4. Indicate on your floor plan which section is North. Fill in the other directions as illustrated. Please note that North can lie in a corner section.

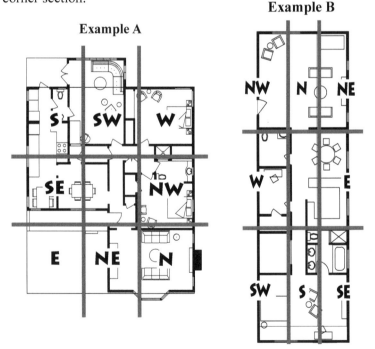

Example A

Example B

DIRECTIONS TO AVOID
FOR CONSTRUCTION 2014

The Three Sha and the Sui Po

The **Three Sha** are in the **North (Northwest and Northeast)**:
Hai, Zi and Chou directions

The **Sui Po** or **Year Breaker** is in the **North**
Zi direction

The **Tai Sui** is in the **South**:
Wu direction.

Therefore, avoid using these directions:
Hai, Ren, Zi, Gui and **Chou**

Directions to Avoid

15° Direction	Degrees	45° Direction	Sang's Luopan Alpha Designation
Hai	322.5 – 337.5	NW	w
Ren			x
Zi	337.5 – 22.5	N	a
Gui			b
Chou	22.5 – 37.5	NE	c

What should we avoid in these directions?

- New construction sitting in these directions.
- Major renovation to buildings sitting in these directions.
- Major renovations to this section of the house, regardless of sitting direction.
- Burial of the deceased in these directions.
- If digging cannot be avoided in any of these areas, then place a metal wind chime outside between the house and digging site. cannot be avoided in any of these areas, then place a metal wind chime outside between the house and digging site.
- In addition, Horses or Rats born in the 1st, 5th or 11th month of the lunar calendar should avoid attending funerals or burials.

FENG SHUI 2014

Qi Pattern

SE **3** Jade	**S** **8** White	**SW** **1** White
E **2** Black	 **4** Green	**W** **6** White
NE **7** Red	**N** **9** Purple	**NW** **5** Yellow

The Qi (energy) shift begins on
February 4th at 6:21 am

INTRODUCTION

While this diagram may look foreign to the beginner, it is essential information for the experienced Feng Shui practitioner. Each year the qi pattern brings different effects. Some of these effects are quite auspicious and favorable and some may be inauspicious and not so favorable.

The effects of the 2014 energy pattern are analyzed for you in the following pages. Each analysis contains suggested remedies or enhancements for each section. Remedies are recommended to reduce negative qi. Enhancements are recommended to increase beneficial qi. These remedies or enhancements consist of the five elements: wood, fire, earth, metal, and water.

To use a remedy or enhancement, it must be placed inside the house within that particular section. If more than one room exists within a section, then each room needs to have its own remedy or enhancement. Any exceptions will be noted.

Feng Shui

FENG SHUI ❧ 2014

SE	S	SW
3 Jade	**8** White	**1** White
E	Literary *Wen Chu*	W
2 Black	**4** Green	**6** White
NE	N	NW
7 Red	**9** Purple	**5** Yellow

The Center Section

Center

Analysis

Last year we predicted that we need to be cautious of all earth-relate disasters during 2013 - earthquakes, fires, landslides, floods, and other extreme weather conditions, economic crisis, political unrest and upheaval, terrorist attacks, and multiple wars would occur.

This year, 2014, the *4 Green Wen Qu Star* visits the Center. It is an auspicious star that is beneficial for literature, scholars, writers, film producers, actors and people whose work relates to the entertainment industry. *The 4 Green Wen Qu Star* is wood element; it is a Peach Blossom romantic star. We are currently in Period 8. This Period 8 belongs to the 8 White Zuo Fu Star. 8 White is of the Earth element. Due to a domination relationship between 4 Green (Wood) and 8 White (Earth) in the center, there is a sign of the danger of breaking down or a setback in real estate or property investment and there are also signs of big scandal in the entertainment industry or for a well-known scholar. This is particularly applicable to those who are young.

In 2014, the *2 Black Sickness Star* falls in the East, so it is not a good year for the Eastern part of the world, such as the Asian countries. People in these areas should be extremely cautious of being attacked by dangerous contagious diseases. Therefore, epidemic diseases such as SARS, bird flu (H7N9) or some other kind of unknown disease is foreseen. Another inauspicious star, the *5 Yellow Disaster Star*, falls in the Northwest. The Northwest is the home of trigram Qian, so this indicates that it is not beneficial for leadership and is a sign of danger for political leaders. Moreover, there should be extra caution for transportation-related disasters.

Feng Shui

FENG SHUI 2014

SE	S	SW
☴ **3** Jade	☷ **8** White	☶ **1** White
E Sickness *Ju Men* ☵ **2** Black	**4** Green	W ☲ **6** White
NE ☶ **7** Red	N ☳ **9** Purple	NW ☰ **5** Yellow

The East Section

East

Situation

Doors, bedrooms, study rooms in the East Section.

Analysis

The *2 Black Sickness Ju Men Star* is in the East section in 2014. Its element is earth. This 2 Black Star is beneficial for medicine, doctors, attorneys and women's rights. But the 2 Black Star also represents sickness, gossip and misunderstandings during the current Period 8 (from 2004 to 2023). The East section is the home of the 3 Jade Lu Cun Star, which belong to the wood element. The combination of the wood of 3 Jade and the earth of 2 Black create a 2-3 combination, which is a domination relationship. If the main entrance of the building is in this section, it is not advisable to make any kind of risky investment and contracts should be signed only after careful consideration; otherwise, legal problems will be easily aroused. A bed room in this section is not beneficial, as the occupant may fall sick easily.

Warning:

Lawsuits, sickness, accidents and casualties are easily aroused.

Beneficial

Prosperity for industries involving attorneys or medicine and clinics.

Remedy

Use a metal container filled with water.

Bathroom

SE **Gossip** *Lu Cun* ≡≡ **3** Jade	**S** ≡≡ **8** White	**SW** ≡≡ **1** White
E ≡≡ **2** Black	**4** Green	**W** ≡≡ **6** White
NE ≡≡ **7** Red	**N** ≡≡ **9** Purple	**NW** ≡≡ **5** Yellow

The Southeast Section

red lightlight

Southeast

Situation

Doors, bedrooms, study rooms in the Southeast Section.

Analysis

This year, the Wen Chang Stars and The *3 Lu Cun Star* visit the Southeast together. The 3 Lu Cun Star is wood element; it represents ambition, expansion, promotion gossip, arguments, misunderstandings, and robberies.

The Southeast is the home of 4 Green Wen Qu Star, and its element is also wood. The 4 Green Wen Qu Star brings the potential for romantic affairs and academic achievement. Because the 3 and 4 stars are both wood element, it gives this section auspicious luck for sales, promotion, business expansion, lawyers, psychics, scholars of literature, writers, publishers, and individuals working in the entertainment industry.

To make full use of it: Use fire

A possible fire element enhancement could be a red light bulb or a lamp with red shade, or any decorative item with the red color or its correspondence colors of maroon, purple or fuchsia. Actual fire elements, such as burning candles, is not recommended.

Warning

The section is strong for Peach Blossom, so one can easily encounter extramarital affairs, scandals, arguments, misunderstandings, and robberies.

Feng Shui

FENG SHUI

Bedroom 2014

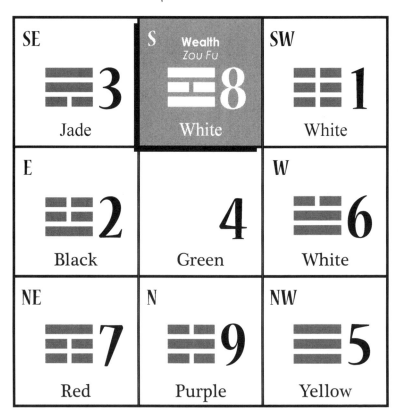

SE	S **Wealth** *Zou Fu*	SW
☴ 3	☵ 8	☷ 1
Jade	White	White
E		W
☷ 2	4	☵ 6
Black	Green	White
NE	N	NW
☶ 7	☶ 9	☰ 5
Red	Purple	Yellow

The South Section

South

Situation

Doors, bedrooms, study rooms in the South Section.

Analysis

In 2014, the **8 White Zuo Fu Wealth Star** arrives in the South along with number of auspicious stars. The 8 White Zuo Fu Star's element is Earth. The 9 Purple Star is in the South section, which brings promotions and celebration. The 9 Purple Star is fire. These two stars, Earth and Fire, have a productive relationship and help this section to produce good money luck, fame, and various kinds of celebration. Spending more time here will be beneficial for teenagers and individuals who work in property investment, real estate, or the landscaping business.

To enhance it: use fire

To enhance your money luck even more, add the earth element with a fire-related color. This could be a decorative piece of glazed pottery or porcelain in red, burgundy, purple, maroon, or even terracotta.

Caution

Not beneficial for water-related businesses.

Feng Shui

FENG SHUI

2014

SE	S	SW **Fortunate** *Tan Lang*
☳ 3	☶ 8	☷ 1
Jade	White	White
E		W
☵ 2	4	☱ 6
Black	Green	White
NE	N	NW
☶ 7	☴ 9	☰ 5
Red	Purple	Yellow

The Southwest Section

Southwest

Situation

Doors, bedrooms, study rooms in the Southwest Section.

Analysis

The *1 White Tan Lang Fortunate Star* visits the Southwest in 2014. The Fortunate Star brings wealth, fame, romance, and good negotiations. The 1 White Star is water element. The 2 Black Ju Men Star is located in the Southwest section. The 2 Black Star is earth. Earth and water have a relationship of domination which creates unharmonious relationships within the family (especially for a couple). Other inauspicious annual stars also fall in the Southwest, so someone who spends a lot of time in this section should be extremely careful of kidney-related illness, blood-related health problems, and sexually transmitted diseases, as well as unfavorable legal affairs.

Warning

Disharmony within the family and sickness are easily aroused. Not beneficial for water-related businesses.

The Remedy: use metal

To reduce the potential negative effects mentioned above, use metal element as a remedy in this section. A metal remedy can consist of some kind of metal décor, such as a piece of sculpture or an ornament, preferably with moving metal parts (for example, a grandfather clock).

FENG SHUI 2014

SE ☷ **3** Jade	**S** ☵ **8** White	**SW** ☶ **1** White
E ☴ **2** Black	**4** Green	**W** Fortunate *Wu Qu* ☱ **6** White
NE ☴ **7** Red	**N** ☳ **9** Purple	**NW** ☲ **5** Yellow

The West Section

West

Situation

Doors, bedrooms, study rooms in the West Section.

Analysis

In 2014 the *6 White Wu Qu Fortunate Star* falls in the West. This auspicious star brings the potential for creativity, wealth, power and authority. The 6 White Star is metal element.

This year auspicious and inauspicious annual stars mix in the West. The West is the home of the 7 Red Po Jun Fighting Star. The 6 White (metal) meeting 7 Red (metal) creates strong metal qi that turns the West into a section where the auspicious and inauspicious mix.

It will be beneficial for military officers, politicians, or individuals working in the financial industry (such as bankers, stock brokers, money lenders), or those in the business of cosmetic products, beauty salons, etc. There is strong money luck.

Warning

One may encounter competition, pressure, and fighting or get injured by sharp metal objects, as well as inharmonious relationships.

Remedy

To reduce the potential negative effects mentioned above, use water to soften the strong metal qi but this will reduce the positive qi as well. Safety first!

Feng Shui

FENG SHUI 2014

SE ☰ **3** Jade	S ☷ **8** White	SW ☷ **1** White
E ☷ **2** Black	**4** Green	W ☵ **6** White
NE ☶ **7** Red	N ☲ **9** Purple	**NW** Disaster *Lian Zhen* ☰ **5** Yellow

The Northwest Section

78

Northwest

Situation

Doors, bedrooms, study rooms in the Northwest Section.

Analysis

The *5 Yellow Lian Zhen Disaster Star* visits the Northwest this year. The Disaster Star brings the potential for delays, obstacles, fire, lawsuits, sickness, and casualty. The 5 Yellow Star is earth element. The Northwest is the home location of the 6 White Fortune Star. Therefore, someone who spends a lot of time in this section should constantly be on guard and refrain from gambling or financial speculation. If your main entrance or bedroom falls in Northwest, stay on high alert. Be careful of conflicts with others, mostly due to challenging authority. Also be on guard for unexpected casualties such as gunshots, bleeding, fire, lawsuits, sickness, or financial losses.

Caution

Financial mishaps, demotions(setback in power or position) and various negative effects mentioned above.

Remedy: use metal

To reduce the potential negative effects mentioned above, use a metal remedy in this section. A metal remedy can consist of some kind of metal sculpture or an ornament, preferably with moving metal parts.

FENG SHUI

2014

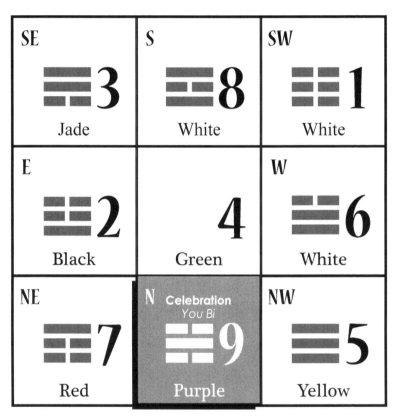

SE ☰≡ 3 Jade	**S** ≡≡ 8 White	**SW** ≡≡ 1 White
E ≡≡ 2 Black	4 Green	**W** ≡≡ 6 White
NE ≡≡ 7 Red	**N** Celebration *You Bi* ≡≡ 9 Purple	**NW** ≡≡ 5 Yellow

The North Section

North

Situation

Doors, bedrooms, study rooms in the North Section.

Analysis

The *9 Purple You Bi Celebration Star* is in the North this year. The 9 Purple Star is fire element and is a star of celebration. The North is related to 1 White Star and is water element. Although the 9 Purple (fire element) and the 1 White (water element) have a domination relationship, the combination of these two auspicious stars still brings this section good potential for fame, receiving honor, romance, marriage, expanding social circles, new creative or trendy businesses, and career advancements. However, this year the three Sha are in the North section and combine with the inauspicious Sui Po star, it is advisable to avoid ground digging or construction in this section since it is easy to arouse misfortune.

Warning

Avoid ground breaking or construction.

Be cautious of public relationships. Exercise caution to avoid big losses due to hasty emotional decisions. Be careful of the eyes or heart-related problems.

Feng Shui

FENG SHUI

2014

SE ≡≡ **3** Jade	**S** ≡≡ **8** White	**SW** ≡≡ **1** White
E ≡≡ **2** Black	**4** Green	**W** ≡≡ **6** White
NE Fighting *Po Jun* ≡≡ **7** Red	**N** ≡≡ **9** Purple	**NW** ≡≡ **5** Yellow

The Northeast Section

Northeast

Situation

Doors, bedrooms, study rooms in the Northeast Section.

Analysis

In 2014, the *7 Red Po Jun Fighting Star* is in the Northeast. The 7 Po Jun Star is a competitive and fighting star but it also brings wealth and promotions. The 7 Red Star's element is metal. The Northeast is the home of the 8 White Zuo Fu Money Star which brings fame and wealth. The 8 White Star is earth. There are other annual auspicious stars combining harmoniously with these two stars, making the Northeast section greatly beneficial for singers, actors, or individuals working in the entertainment or insurance industries and sales. There is strong Peach Blossom for the young.

Warning

There is the danger of getting involved in scandalous affairs. One may encounter competition, pressure, or frustration because of baseless gossip.

Feng Shui

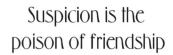

Suspicion is the
poison of friendship

Calligraphy by Larry Sang

DAY SELECTION

DAY SELECTION

Introduction to Day Selection

Day Selection has been used for a long time in China. Every year, almanacs would be published giving the best days for important activities, as well as days to avoid. It is thought that a positive outcome is more likely when an activity is begun on an auspicious day. In English, we talk abut getting things off to a good start, but have no particular methodology to do this.

There are three aspects to selecting a good day: picking a day that is good for the activity, avoiding a day that is bad for the activity, and picking a day that is not bad for the person(s) involved. In the calendar pages that follow, each day will list two or three activities that are auspicious or inauspicious on that day. If you wanted to pick a date to get married, you would first look for the days that were considered good for weddings. In addition, you need to check the birth information of the bride and groom. If the bride is a Rabbit and the groom is a Rat, then you also need to avoid any days that say Bad for Rat or Bad for Rabbit, even if they are good for weddings in general.

In addition, there are some days that are not good for any important activity. Usually this is because the energy of heaven and earth is too strong or inharmonious on those days.

Day Selection is used for the first day of an activity. It does not affect a continued activity. For example, you should begin construction on a day that is good for ground breaking, but it is not a problem if the construction is continued through a day that is bad for ground breaking. The construction need not be stopped.

On the next page are definitions of the various activities included in Master Sang's Day Selection Calendar.

CALENDAR TERMINOLOGY KEY

Animals:
Generally a bad day for a person born in the year of the animal listed. Even if an activity is listed as beneficial for that day, it will usually not be beneficial for that animal.

*Begin Mission:
Beginning a new position, mission, or assignment.

Burial:
Burial.

*Business:
Trade or business.

*Buy Property:
Purchasing real estate.

*Construction:
Begin work on buildings, roads, etc.

*Contracts:
Signing or entering into a contract, pact, or agreement.

Don't Do Important Things:
A bad day for most activities.

Fix House:
Reprairing the inside or outside of the house. Also for installing major appliances, such as the stove or oven.

Funeral:
Funerals.

*Grand Opening:
Opening a new business, restaurant, etc. Opening ceremonies for a new event.

Ground Breaking:
Beginning construction or disturbing the earth.

Ground Digging:
Unearth or excavate the earth with a shovel or spade to remove material or plants.

Hunting:
To chase wild animals for the purpose of catching or killing

Lawsuit:
Filing a lawsuit or going to court.

*Moving:
Moving or changing residences.

Planting:
Gardening or planting.

Prayer:
Praying for blessings or happiness.

School:
Admissions into a new school.

Surgery:
Medical treatment or operation.

*Travel:
Going out or beginning a trip.

*Wedding:
Marriage ceremonies or becoming engaged to be married.

Worship:
Rituals, rites, ceremonies, offering sacrifices, or honoring ancestors or the dead.

Most Activities:
Includes all activities marked (*)

S	M	T	W	T	F	S
			1	2	3	4
5	6	7	8	9	10	11
12	13	14	15	16	17	18
19	20	21	22	23	24	25
26	27	28	29	30	31	

January 2014

unfavorable for:

Day	Details	Sign
Wed **1**	**Good for:** prayer worship, school ***Bad for:*** *wedding, grand opening*	*Tiger*
Thu **2**	**Good for:** contruction, contracts, business ***Bad for:*** *burial, fix house*	*Rabbit*
Fri **3**	**Good for:** grand opening, wedding, moving ***Bad for:*** *hunting, ground digging*	*Dragon*
Sat **4**	⊖ **DON'T DO IMPORTANT THINGS** ⊖	*Snake*
Sun **5**	**Good for:** prayer, worship, school ***Bad for:*** *begin mission, travel*	*Horse*
Mon **6**	**Good for:** business, travel, contracts ***Bad for:*** *burial, fix house*	*Sheep*
Tue **7**	**Good for:** wedding, grand opening, business ***Bad for:*** *hunting, ground digging*	*Monkey*
Wed **8**	**Good for:** school, moving, begin mission ***Bad for:*** *burial, ground breaking*	*Rooster*
Thu **9**	**Good for:** wedding, begin mission, travel ***Bad for:*** *hunting, burial*	*Dog*
Fri **10**	**Good for:** business, travel, contracts ***Bad for:*** *surgery, lawsuit*	*Pig*
Sat **11**	**Good for:** worship, travel, ground digging ***Bad for:*** *grand opening, begin mission*	*Rat*
Sun **12**	⊖ **DON'T DO IMPORTANT THINGS** ⊖	*Ox*
Mon **13**	**Good for:** school, moving, begin mission ***Bad for:*** *contracts, begin mission*	*Tiger*
Tue **14**	**Good for:** prayer, worship, school ***Bad for:*** *burial, fix house*	*Rabbit*
Wed **15**	**Good for:** worship, house cleaning, planting ***Bad for:*** *begin mission, travel*	*Dragon*

Date		Activities		Zodiac
Thu **16**		⊖ **DON'T DO IMPORTANT THINGS** ⊖		*Snake*
Fri **17**		**Good for:** business, travel, contracts *Bad for: burial, fix house*		*Horse*
Sat **18**		**Good for:** contracts, business, school *Bad for: hunting, surgery*		*Sheep*
Sun **19**		**Good for:** wedding, grand opening, business *Bad for: burial, ground breaking*		*Monkey*
Mon **20**		**Good for:** wedding, begin mission, travel *Bad for: surgery, funeral*		*Rooster*
Tue **21**		**Good for:** burial, ground breaking, worship *Bad for: grand opening, begin mission*		*Dog*
Wed **22**		**Good for:** wedding, contracts, construction *Bad for: burial, ground breaking*		*Pig*
Thu **23**		**Good for:** house cleaning, planting *Bad for: wedding, contracts, business*		*Rat*
Fri **24**		⊖ **DON'T DO IMPORTANT THINGS** ⊖		*Ox*
Sat **25**		**Good for:** worship, prayer, house cleaning *Bad for: buy property, ground breaking*		*Tiger*
Sun **26**		**Good for:** school, wedding, grand opening *Bad for: surgery, funeral*		*Rabbit*
Mon **27**		**Good for:** hunting, planting, school *Bad for: burial, fix house*		*Dragon*
Tue **28**		⊖ **DON'T DO IMPORTANT THINGS** ⊖		*Snake*
Wed **29**		**Good for:** worship, business, house cleaning *Bad for: hunting, lawsuit*		*Horse*
Thu **30**		**Good for:** wedding, grand opening, business *Bad for: burial, fix house, ground breaking*		*Sheep*
Fri **31**		**Good for:** house cleaning, prayer *Bad for: begin mission, travel*		*Monkey*

February 2014

Day	Details	Unfavorable for
Sat 1	**Good for:** wedding, grand opening, business ***Bad for:*** *burial, fix house, ground breaking*	*Rooster*
Sun 2	**Good for:** worship, prayer, house cleaning ***Bad for:*** *grand opening, begin mission*	*Dog*
Mon 3	⊖ **DON'T DO IMPORTANT THINGS** ⊖	*Pig*
Tue 4	**Good for:** wedding, grand opening, business ***Bad for:*** *funeral, burial*	*Rat*
Wed 5	**Good for:** wedding, contracts, grand opening ***Bad for:*** *ground digging, hunting*	*Ox*
Thu 6	**Good for:** travel, moving ***Bad for:*** *wedding, business*	*Tiger*
Fri 7	**Good for:** worship, prayer, house cleaning ***Bad for:*** *grand opening, begin mission*	*Rabbit*
Sat 8	**Good for:** worship, prayer ***Bad for:*** *wedding, grand opening*	*Dragon*
Sun 9	**Good for:** wedding, grand opening, contracts ***Bad for:*** *burial, hunting*	*Snake*
Mon 10	⊖ **DON'T DO IMPORTANT THINGS** ⊖	*Horse*
Tue 11	**Good for:** worship, prayer ***Bad for:*** *wedding, grand opening*	*Sheep*
Wed 12	**Good for:** worship, planting ***Bad for:*** *grand opening, begin mission*	*Monkey*
Thu 13	**Good for:** ground breaking, business ***Bad for:*** *wedding, begin mission*	*Rooster*
Fri 14	**Good for:** wedding, grand opening, business ***Bad for:*** *funeral, burial*	*Dog*

S M T W T F S

2 3 4 5 6 7 8
9 10 11 12 13 14 15
16 17 18 19 20 21 22
23 24 25 26 27 28

Sat **15**	**Good for:** worship, prayer **Bad for:** grand opening, begin mission		*Pig*
Sun **16**	**Good for:** wedding, grand opening, begin mission **Bad for:** funeral, lawsuit		*Rat*
Mon **17**	**Good for:** worship, prayer **Bad for:** business, contracts		*Ox*
Tue **18**	⊖ **DON'T DO IMPORTANT THINGS** ⊖		*Tiger*
Wed **19**	**Good for:** worship, planting **Bad for:** grand opening, begin mission		*Rabbit*
Thu **20**	**Good for:** begin mission, grand opening, contracts **Bad for:** funeral, burial		*Dragon*
Fri **21**	**Good for:** worship, prayer **Bad for:** business, contracts		*Snake*
Sat **22**	⊖ **DON'T DO IMPORTANT THINGS** ⊖		*Horse*
Sun **23**	**Good for:** house cleaning, worship **Bad for:** grand opening, business		*Sheep*
Mon **24**	**Good for:** contracts, business **Bad for:** funeral, ground digging		*Monkey*
Tue **25**	**Good for:** wedding, grand opening, begin mission **Bad for:** funeral, lawsuit		*Rooster*
Wed **26**	**Good for:** worship, prayer **Bad for:** wedding, grand opening		*Dog*
Thu **27**	**Good for:** house cleaning, worship **Bad for:** grand opening, begin mission		*Pig*
Fri **28**	**Good for:** wedding, grand opening, buy property **Bad for:** funeral, burial		*Rat*

S	M	T	W	T	F	S
						1
2	3	4	5	6	7	8
9	10	11	12	13	14	15
16	17	18	19	20	21	22
23	24	25	26	27	28	29
30	31					

March 2014

unfavorable for:

Day		Good/Bad	Animal
Sat **1**		**Good for:** begin mission, grand opening, contracts ***Bad for:*** *funeral, lawsuit*	Ox
Sun **2**		**Good for:** worship, prayer ***Bad for:*** *grand opening, business*	Tiger
Mon **3**		**Good for:** prayer, worship, burial ***Bad for:*** *business, begin mission*	Rabbit
Tue **4**		**Good for:** house cleaning, worship ***Bad for:*** *business, contracts, begin mission*	Dragon
Wed **5**		**Good for:** begin mission, grand opening, contracts ***Bad for:*** *funeral, burial, ground digging*	Snake
Thu **6**		⚊ **DON'T DO IMPORTANT THINGS** ⚊	Horse
Fri **7**		**Good for:** wedding, grand opening, buy property ***Bad for:*** *funeral, lawsuit*	Sheep
Sat **8**		**Good for:** house cleaning, worship ***Bad for:*** *wedding, grand opening*	Monkey
Sun **9**		**Good for:** worship, prayer ***Bad for:*** *business, begin mission*	Rooster
Mon **10**		**Good for:** house cleaning, worship ***Bad for:*** *business, contracts, begin mission*	Dog
Tue **11**		**Good for:** begin mission, grand opening, contracts ***Bad for:*** *funeral, lawsuit*	Pig
Wed **12**		**Good for:** worship, prayer ***Bad for:*** *business, begin mission*	Rat
Thu **13**		**Good for:** wedding, grand opening, buy property ***Bad for:*** *hunting, lawsuit*	Ox
Fri **14**		**Good for:** house cleaning, worship ***Bad for:*** *wedding, grand opening*	Tiger
Sat **15**		⚊ **DON'T DO IMPORTANT THINGS** ⚊	Rabbit

Sun **16**	**Good for:** worship, prayer *Bad for: business, begin mission*	*Dragon*
Mon **17**	**Good for:** house cleaning, worship *Bad for: wedding, grand opening*	*Snake*
Tue **18**	⊖ **DON'T DO IMPORTANT THINGS** ⊖	*Horse*
Wed **19**	**Good for:** wedding, grand opening, buy property *Bad for: funeral, lawsuit*	*Sheep*
Thu **20**	⊖ **DON'T DO IMPORTANT THINGS** ⊖	*Monkey*
Fri **21**	**Good for:** worship, prayer *Bad for: business, contracts, begin mission*	*Rooster*
Sat **22**	**Good for:** business, begin mission, buy property *Bad for: funeral, burial, ground digging*	*Dog*
Sun **23**	**Good for:** contracts, business, buy property *Bad for: burial, ground digging*	*Pig*
Mon **24**	**Good for:** worship, prayer *Bad for: wedding, grand opening*	*Rat*
Tue **25**	**Good for:** worship, prayer, school *Bad for: business, contracts*	*Ox*
Wed **26**	**Good for:** house fixing, worship, prayer *Bad for: begin mission, travel*	*Tiger*
Thu **27**	⊖ **DON'T DO IMPORTANT THINGS** ⊖	*Rabbit*
Fri **28**	**Good for:** worship, prayer *Bad for: most activities*	*Dragon*
Sat **29**	**Good for:** most activities *Bad for: funeral, lawsuit*	*Snake*
Sun **30**	⊖ **DON'T DO IMPORTANT THINGS** ⊖	*Horse*
Mon **31**	**Good for:** wedding, grand opening, buy property *Bad for: funeral, lawsuit*	*Sheep*

S	M	T	W	T	F	S
	1	2	3	4	5	6
7	8	9	10	11	12	13
14	15	16	17	18	19	20
21	22	23	24	25	26	27
28	29	30				

April 2014

unfavorable for:

Day	Activities	Unfavorable
Tue **1**	**Good for:** house fixing, worship, prayer **Bad for:** begin mission, travel	Monkey
Wed **2**	**Good for:** worship, prayer, school **Bad for:** business, contracts	Rooster
Thu **3**	**Good for:** most activities **Bad for:** funeral, burial, ground digging	Dog
Fri **4**	**Good for:** worship, prayer, contracts **Bad for:** begin mission, travel	Pig
Sat **5**	**Good for:** prayer, worship **Bad for:** grand opening, wedding	Rat
Sun **6**	**Good for:** worship, school, contracts **Bad for:** begin mission, grand opening	Ox
Mon **7**	**Good for:** worship, prayer **Bad for:** business, contracts	Tiger
Tue **8**	**Good for:** wedding, grand opening, buy property **Bad for:** ground digging, moving	Rabbit
Wed **9**	**Good for:** worship, prayer, planting **Bad for:** begin mission, travel	Dragon
Thu **10**	**Good for:** planting, school, contracts **Bad for:** funeral, lawsuit	Snake
Fri **11**	⊖ **DON'T DO IMPORTANT THINGS** ⊖	Horse
Sat **12**	**Good for:** worship, prayer **Bad for:** most activities	Sheep
Sun **13**	**Good for:** most activities **Bad for:** funeral, lawsuit	Monkey
Mon **14**	**Good for:** worship, prayer **Bad for:** most activities	Rooster
Tue **15**	**Good for:** worship, prayer **Bad for:** wedding, grand opening	Dog

Wed **16**	**Good for:** most activities *Bad for: funeral, burial, ground digging*	*Pig*
Thu **17**	**Good for:** worship, prayer, planting *Bad for: begin mission, travel*	*Rat*
Fri **18**	**Good for:** planting, school, contracts *Bad for: most activities*	*Ox*
Sat **19**	**Good for:** prayer *Bad for: most activities*	*Tiger*
Sun **20**	**Good for:** planting, school, contracts *Bad for: funeral, lawsuit*	*Rabbit*
Mon **21**	⊖ **DON'T DO IMPORTANT THINGS** ⊖	*Dragon*
Tue **22**	**Good for:** worship, prayer *Bad for: Bad for: most activities*	*Snake*
Wed **23**	⊖ **DON'T DO IMPORTANT THINGS** ⊖	*Horse*
Thu **24**	**Good for:** worship, prayer, planting *Bad for: begin mission, travel*	*Sheep*
Fri **25**	**Good for:** planting, school, contracts *Bad for: ground digging, moving*	*Monkey*
Sat **26**	**Good for:** worship, prayer *Bad for: wedding, grand opening*	*Rooster*
Sun **27**	**Good for:** worship, prayer *Bad for: most activities*	*Dog*
Mon **28**	**Good for:** prayer *Bad for: begin mission, grand opening*	*Pig*
Tue **29**	**Good for:** worship, prayer *Bad for: wedding, grand opening*	*Rat*
Wed **30**	**Good for:** worship, prayer, planting *Bad for: lawsuit*	*Ox*

May 2014

Thu **1**	**Good for:** worship, ground breaking ***Bad for:*** *begin mission, travel*	*Tiger*
Fri **2**	**Good for:** wedding, grand opening, buy property ***Bad for:*** *funeral, lawsuit, burial*	*Rabbit*
Sat **3**	⊖ **DON'T DO IMPORTANT THINGS** ⊖	*Dragon*
Sun **4**	**Good for:** worship, prayer ***Bad for:*** *most activities*	*Snake*
Mon **5**	⊖ **DON'T DO IMPORTANT THINGS** ⊖	*Horse*
Tue **6**	**Good for:** wedding, grand opening, buy property ***Bad for:*** *funeral, lawsuit, burial*	*Sheep*
Wed **7**	**Good for:** worship, prayer ***Bad for:*** *most activities*	*Monkey*
Thu **8**	**Good for:** worship, prayer, school ***Bad for:*** *business, grand opening*	*Rooster*
Fri **9**	**Good for:** worship, prayer ***Bad for:*** *most activities*	*Dog*
Sat **10**	**Good for:** wedding, grand opening, moving ***Bad for:*** *funeral, lawsuit, burial*	*Pig*
Sun **11**	**Good for:** worship, prayer, school ***Bad for:*** *wedding, grand opening*	*Rat*
Mon **12**	**Good for:** worship, prayer ***Bad for:*** *most activities*	*Ox*
Tue **13**	**Good for:** most activities ***Bad for:*** *funeral, lawsuit, burial*	*Tiger*
Wed **14**	**Good for:** wedding, grand opening, business ***Bad for:*** *ground digging, hunting*	*Rabbit*
Thu **15**	**Good for:** worship, prayer ***Bad for:*** *most activities*	*Dragon*

Fri **16**	⊖ **DON'T DO IMPORTANT THINGS** ⊖	*Snake*
Sat **17**	⊖ **DON'T DO IMPORTANT THINGS** ⊖	*Horse*
Sun **18**	**Good for:** begin mission, grand opening, business *Bad for: funeral, burial, ground digging*	*Sheep*
Mon **19**	**Good for:** wedding, grand opening, moving *Bad for: ground digging, hunting*	*Monkey*
Tue **20**	**Good for:** most activities *Bad for: ground digging, hunting*	*Rooster*
Wed **21**	**Good for:** worship, prayer *Bad for: most activities*	*Dog*
Thu **22**	**Good for:** begin mission, school *Bad for: business, ground breaking*	*Pig*
Fri **23**	**Good for:** most activities *Bad for: ground digging*	*Rat*
Sat **24**	**Good for:** worship, prayer *Bad for: most activities*	*Ox*
Sun **25**	**Good for:** begin mission, school, wedding *Bad for: ground digging, hunting*	*Tiger*
Mon **26**	**Good for:** most activities *Bad for: ground digging*	*Rabbit*
Tue **27**	**Good for:** begin mission, grand opening, business *Bad for: funeral, burial, ground digging*	*Dragon*
Wed **28**	⊖ **DON'T DO IMPORTANT THINGS** ⊖	*Snake*
Thu **29**	⊖ **DON'T DO IMPORTANT THINGS** ⊖	*Horse*
Fri **30**	**Good for:** most activities *Bad for: ground breaking*	*Sheep*
Sat **31**	**Good for:** worship, prayer *Bad for: most activities*	*Monkey*

June 2014

unfavorable for:

Day		Unfavorable
Sun **1**	**Good for:** worship, prayer, school ***Bad for:*** *business, contracts, buy property*	*Rooster*
Mon **2**	**Good for:** worship, prayer ***Bad for:*** *most activities*	*Dog*
Tue **3**	**Good for:** wedding, grand opening, business ***Bad for:*** *funeral, burial, ground digging*	*Pig*
Wed **4**	**Good for:** worship, prayer ***Bad for:*** *most activities*	*Rat*
Thu **5**	**Good for:** worship, prayer ***Bad for:*** *most activities*	*Ox*
Fri **6**	**Good for:** most activities ***Bad for:*** *lawsuit, hunting*	*Tiger*
Sat **7**	**Good for:** worship, prayer ***Bad for:*** *business, contracts, buy property*	*Rabbit*
Sun **8**	**Good for:** most activities ***Bad for:*** *lawsuit, hunting*	*Dragon*
Mon **9**	**Good for:** prayer, worship ***Bad for:*** *most activities*	*Snake*
Tue **10**	⊖ **DON'T DO IMPORTANT THINGS** ⊖	*Horse*
Wed **11**	**Good for:** worship, prayer ***Bad for:*** *most activities*	*Sheep*
Thu **12**	**Good for:** most activities ***Bad for:*** *lawsuit, hunting*	*Monkey*
Fri **13**	**Good for:** worship, prayer, planting ***Bad for:*** *business, contracts*	*Rooster*
Sat **14**	**Good for:** wedding, grand opening, business ***Bad for:*** *funeral, burial, ground digging*	*Dog*
Sun **15**	**Good for:** worship, prayer, planting ***Bad for:*** *most activities*	*Pig*

Day	Activities	Zodiac
Mon **16**	**Good for:** worship, prayer ***Bad for:*** *most activities*	*Rat*
Tue **17**	⊖ **DON'T DO IMPORTANT THINGS** ⊖	*Ox*
Wed **18**	**Good for:** begin mission, school, moving ***Bad for:*** *ground digging, hunting, fix house*	*Tiger*
Thu **19**	⊖ **DON'T DO IMPORTANT THINGS** ⊖	*Rabbit*
Fri **20**	**Good for:** most activities ***Bad for:*** *lawsuit, hunting*	*Dragon*
Sat **21**	**Good for:** worship, prayer, planting ***Bad for:*** *most activities*	*Snake*
Sun **22**	⊖ **DON'T DO IMPORTANT THINGS** ⊖	*Horse*
Mon **23**	**Good for:** worship, prayer ***Bad for:*** *most activities*	*Sheep*
Tue **24**	**Good for:** most activities ***Bad for:*** *ground digging, hunting, fix house*	*Monkey*
Wed **25**	**Good for:** worship, prayer ***Bad for:*** *most activities*	*Rooster*
Thu **26**	**Good for:** begin mission, fix house, moving ***Bad for:*** *funeral, burial*	*Dog*
Fri **27**	**Good for:** worship, prayer, planting ***Bad for:*** *business, contracts, buy property*	*Pig*
Sat **28**	**Good for:** worship, prayer ***Bad for:*** *most activities*	*Rat*
Sun **29**	**Good for:** most activities ***Bad for:*** *burial, ground breaking*	*Ox*
Mon **30**	**Good for:** worship, prayer, planting ***Bad for:*** *most activities*	*Tiger*

S	M	T	W	T	F	S
		1	2	3	4	5
6	7	8	9	10	11	12
13	14	15	16	17	18	19
20	21	22	23	24	25	26
27	28	29	30	31		

July 2014

unfavorable for:

Day	Activities	Unfavorable for
Tue 1	⊖ **DON'T DO IMPORTANT THINGS** ⊖	*Rabbit*
Wed 2	**Good for:** most activities ***Bad for:*** *lawsuit, hunting*	*Dragon*
Thu 3	**Good for:** worship, prayer, school ***Bad for:*** *business, contracts, grand opening*	*Snake*
Fri 4	⊖ **DON'T DO IMPORTANT THINGS** ⊖	*Horse*
Sat 5	**Good for:** worship, prayer ***Bad for:*** *most activities*	*Sheep*
Sun 6	**Good for:** most activities ***Bad for:*** *lawsuit, hunting*	*Monkey*
Mon 7	**Good for:** most activities ***Bad for:*** *funeral, burial*	*Rooster*
Tue 8	**Good for:** worship, prayer, planting ***Bad for:*** *most activities*	*Dog*
Wed 9	**Good for:** worship, begin mission, school ***Bad for:*** *business, contracts, buy property*	*Pig*
Thu 10	**Good for:** worship, ground breaking, burial ***Bad for:*** *begin mission, contracts, grand opening*	*Rat*
Fri 11	**Good for:** worship, house cleaning, moving ***Bad for:*** *wedding, grand opening*	*Ox*
Sat 12	**Good for:** most activities ***Bad for:*** *burial, ground breaking*	*Tiger*
Sun 13	**Good for:** worship, prayer ***Bad for:*** *most activities*	*Rabbit*
Mon 14	**Good for:** worship, prayer, planting ***Bad for:*** *most activities*	*Dragon*
Tue 15	**Good for:** fix house, planting, school ***Bad for:*** *begin mission, contracts, grand opening*	*Snake*

Wed **16**	⊖ **DON'T DO IMPORTANT THINGS** ⊖	*Horse*
Thu **17**	**Good for:** worship, prayer, planting *Bad for: most activities*	*Sheep*
Fri **18**	**Good for:** begin mission, grand opening, business *Bad for: moving, contracts, buy property*	*Monkey*
Sat **19**	**Good for:** most activities *Bad for: burial, ground breaking*	*Rooster*
Sun **20**	**Good for:** worship, house cleaning, moving *Bad for: wedding, grand opening*	*Dog*
Mon **21**	**Good for:** worship, begin mission, school *Bad for: business, contracts, buy property*	*Pig*
Tue **22**	**Good for:** worship, ground breaking, burial *Bad for: begin mission, grand opening*	*Rat*
Wed **23**	⊖ **DON'T DO IMPORTANT THINGS** ⊖	*Ox*
Thu **24**	**Good for:** worship, house cleaning, moving *Bad for: begin mission, contracts, grand opening*	*Tiger*
Fri **25**	**Good for:** worship, house cleaning *Bad for: most activities*	*Rabbit*
Sat **26**	**Good for:** worship, prayer *Bad for: wedding, grand opening*	*Dragon*
Sun **27**	**Good for:** most activities *Bad for: burial, ground breaking*	*Snake*
Mon **28**	⊖ **DON'T DO IMPORTANT THINGS** ⊖	*Horse*
Tue **29**	**Good for:** worship, house cleaning *Bad for: most activities*	*Sheep*
Wed **30**	**Good for:** wedding, grand opening, most activities *Bad for: cleaning house, fix house*	*Monkey*
Thu **31**	**Good for:** most activities *Bad for: burial, ground breaking*	*Rooster*

August 2014

unfavorable for:

Fri **1**	**Good for:** wedding, grand opening, begin mission *Bad for: funeral, burial, ground digging*	*Dog*
Sat **2**	**Good for:** worship, begin mission, school *Bad for: business, contracts, buy property*	*Pig*
Sun **3**	**Good for:** worship, prayer *Bad for: most activities*	*Rat*
Mon **4**	⊖ **DON'T DO IMPORTANT THINGS** ⊖	*Ox*
Tue **5**	**Good for:** worship, prayer, moving *Bad for: business, contracts, buy property*	*Tiger*
Wed **6**	**Good for:** worship, prayer *Bad for: most activities*	*Rabbit*
Thu **7**	**Good for:** worship, prayer, planting *Bad for: most activities*	*Dragon*
Fri **8**	**Good for:** worship, prayer *Bad for: business, contracts, buy property*	*Snake*
Sat **9**	⊖ **DON'T DO IMPORTANT THINGS** ⊖	*Horse*
Sun **10**	**Good for:** worship, begin mission, school *Bad for: contracts, grand opening*	*Sheep*
Mon **11**	**Good for:** worship, prayer *Bad for: most activities*	*Monkey*
Tue **12**	**Good for:** worship, house cleaning *Bad for: most activities*	*Rooster*
Wed **13**	**Good for:** worship, begin mission, school *Bad for: funeral, burial, ground digging*	*Dog*
Thu **14**	**Good for:** most activities *Bad for: burial, ground digging*	*Pig*
Fri **15**	**Good for:** most activities *Bad for: burial, lawsuit*	*Rat*

Sat 16	⊖ **DON'T DO IMPORTANT THINGS** ⊖	*Ox*
Sun 17	**Good for:** worship, begin mission, school ***Bad for:*** *most activities*	*Tiger*
Mon 18	**Good for:** worship, burial, planting ***Bad for:*** *business, contracts, buy property*	*Rabbit*
Tue 19	**Good for:** most activities ***Bad for:*** *funeral, burial, ground digging*	*Dragon*
Wed 20	**Good for:** worship, prayer ***Bad for:*** *most activities*	*Snake*
Thu 21	⊖ **DON'T DO IMPORTANT THINGS** ⊖	*Horse*
Fri 22	**Good for:** house cleaning, planting ***Bad for:*** *most activities*	*Sheep*
Sat 23	⊖ **DON'T DO IMPORTANT THINGS** ⊖	*Monkey*
Sun 24	**Good for:** most activities ***Bad for:*** *burial, ground digging*	*Rooster*
Mon 25	**Good for:** wedding, grand opening, most activities ***Bad for:*** *funeral, hunting*	*Dog*
Tue 26	**Good for:** most activities ***Bad for:*** *funeral, fix house*	*Pig*
Wed 27	**Good for:** worship, begin mission, school ***Bad for:*** *most activities*	*Rat*
Thu 28	⊖ **DON'T DO IMPORTANT THINGS** ⊖	*Ox*
Fri 29	**Good for:** most activities ***Bad for:*** *burial, ground digging*	*Tiger*
Sat 30	**Good for:** grand opening, most activities ***Bad for:*** *ground digging*	*Rabbit*
Sun 31	**Good for:** worship, burial, planting ***Bad for:*** *business, contracts, buy property*	*Dragon*

S	M	T	W	T	F	S
	1	2	3	4	5	6
7	8	9	10	11	12	13
14	15	16	17	18	19	20
21	22	23	24	25	26	27
28	29	30				

September 2014

unfavorable for:

Mon **1**	**Good for:** worship, prayer ***Bad for:*** *most activities*	*Snake*
Tue **2**	⊖ **DON'T DO IMPORTANT THINGS** ⊖	*Horse*
Wed **3**	**Good for:** wedding, begin mission, contracts ***Bad for:*** *funeral, hunting*	*Sheep*
Thu **4**	⊖ **DON'T DO IMPORTANT THINGS** ⊖	*Monkey*
Fri **5**	**Good for:** worship, prayer ***Bad for:*** *most activities*	*Rooster*
Sat **6**	**Good for:** prayer ***Bad for:*** *most activities*	*Dog*
Sun **7**	**Good for:** worship ***Bad for:*** *business, buy property*	*Pig*
Mon **8**	**Good for:** most activities ***Bad for:*** *ground digging*	*Rat*
Tue **9**	**Good for:** worship, prayer, school, business ***Bad for:*** *burial, ground digging*	*Ox*
Wed **10**	**Good for:** worship, prayer, burial ***Bad for:*** *most activities*	*Tiger*
Thu **11**	**Good for:** worship, prayer, planting ***Bad for:*** *business, contracts, buy property*	*Rabbit*
Fri **12**	**Good for:** prayer, planting, begin mission ***Bad for:*** *wedding, grand opening*	*Dragon*
Sat **13**	**Good for:** begin mission, contracts, business ***Bad for:*** *burial, ground digging*	*Snake*
Sun **14**	⊖ **DON'T DO IMPORTANT THINGS** ⊖	*Horse*
Mon **15**	**Good for:** worship, prayer ***Bad for:*** *business, buy property*	*Sheep*

Tue **16**	**Good for:** worship, prayer *Bad for: most activities*	*Monkey*
Wed **17**	⊖ **DON'T DO IMPORTANT THINGS** ⊖	*Rooster*
Thu **18**	**Good for:** worship, prayer *Bad for: wedding, grand opening*	*Dog*
Fri **19**	**Good for:** most activities *Bad for: burial, ground digging*	*Pig*
Sat **20**	**Good for:** worship, prayer *Bad for: most activities*	*Rat*
Sun **21**	**Good for:** wedding, begin mission, contracts *Bad for: grand opening, business*	*Ox*
Mon **22**	**Good for:** worship, prayer, burial *Bad for: most activities*	*Tiger*
Tue **23**	**Good for:** worship, prayer *Bad for: wedding, grand opening*	*Rabbit*
Wed **24**	**Good for:** begin mission, contracts, moving *Bad for: business, buy property*	*Dragon*
Thu **25**	**Good for:** grand opening, contracts, business *Bad for: ground digging, fix house*	*Snake*
Fri **26**	⊖ **DON'T DO IMPORTANT THINGS** ⊖	*Horse*
Sat **27**	**Good for:** worship, prayer *Bad for: most activities*	*Sheep*
Sun **28**	⊖ **DON'T DO IMPORTANT THINGS** ⊖	*Monkey*
Mon **29**	**Good for:** prayer *Bad for: most activities*	*Rooster*
Tue **30**	**Good for:** prayer *Bad for: most activities*	*Dog*

9

October 2014

Wed **1**	**Good for:** most activities ***Bad for:*** *ground digging*	*Pig*
Thu **2**	**Good for:** worship, prayer, planting ***Bad for:*** *most activities*	*Rat*
Fri **3**	**Good for:** grand opening, contracts, business ***Bad for:*** *ground digging, fix house*	*Ox*
Sat **4**	**Good for:** contracts, moving, business ***Bad for:*** *ground digging, burial*	*Tiger*
Sun **5**	**Good for:** worship, prayer ***Bad for:*** *most activities*	*Rabbit*
Mon **6**	**Good for:** most activities ***Bad for:*** *ground digging, hunting*	*Dragon*
Tue **7**	**Good for:** worship, prayer, planting ***Bad for:*** *most activities*	*Snake*
Wed **8**	⊖ **DON'T DO IMPORTANT THINGS** ⊖	*Horse*
Thu **9**	**Good for:** worship, prayer ***Bad for:*** *most activities*	*Sheep*
Fri **10**	**Good for:** worship, prayer, planting ***Bad for:*** *most activities*	*Monkey*
Sat **11**	**Good for:** worship, prayer ***Bad for:*** *ground digging, fix house*	*Rooster*
Sun **12**	**Good for:** worship, prayer, planting ***Bad for:*** *most activities*	*Dog*
Mon **13**	**Good for:** worship, prayer ***Bad for:*** *most activities*	*Pig*
Tue **14**	**Good for:** grand opening, begin mission, contracts ***Bad for:*** *ground digging, burial*	*Rat*
Wed **15**	**Good for:** worship, prayer, planting ***Bad for:*** *most activities*	*Ox*

Day	Description	Zodiac
Thu **16**	**Good for:** worship, prayer *Bad for: ground digging*	*Tiger*
Fri **17**	**Good for:** worship, prayer *Bad for: most activities*	*Rabbit*
Sat **18**	**Good for:** prayer, worship *Bad for: ground digging, fix house*	*Dragon*
Sun **19**	**Good for:** worship, prayer *Bad for: most activities*	*Snake*
Mon **20**	⊖ **DON'T DO IMPORTANT THINGS** ⊖	*Horse*
Tue **21**	**Good for:** prayer *Bad for: most activities*	*Sheep*
Wed **22**	**Good for:** worship, prayer *Bad for: most activites*	*Monkey*
Thu **23**	**Good for:** wedding, begin mission, contracts *Bad for: ground digging*	*Rooster*
Fri **24**	**Good for:** prayer *Bad for: most activities*	*Dog*
Sat **25**	**Good for:** worship, prayer, planting *Bad for: wedding, grand opening*	*Pig*
Sun **26**	**Good for:** wedding, grand opening, contracts *Bad for: ground digging, burial*	*Rat*
Mon **27**	**Good for:** business, contracts *Bad for: ground digging, burial*	*Ox*
Tue **28**	**Good for:** worship, prayer *Bad for: business, buy property*	*Tiger*
Wed **29**	**Good for:** prayer *Bad for: most activities*	*Rabbit*
Thu **30**	⊖ **DON'T DO IMPORTANT THINGS** ⊖	*Dragon* 10
Fri **31**	**Good for:** prayer *Bad for: most activities*	*Snake*

unfavorable for:

Sat **1**	⚊ **DON'T DO IMPORTANT THINGS** ⚊	*Horse*
Sun **2**	**Good for:** worship, prayer, planting *Bad for: most activities*	*Sheep*
Mon **3**	**Good for:** worship, prayer *Bad for: ground digging, burial*	*Monkey*
Tue **4**	**Good for:** wedding, grand opening, contracts *Bad for: ground digging, fix house*	*Rooster*
Wed **5**	**Good for:** worship, prayer *Bad for: most activities*	*Dog*
Thu **6**	**Good for:** most activities *Bad for: ground digging, burial*	*Pig*
Fri **7**	**Good for:** worship, prayer *Bad for: lawsuit, fix house, grand opening*	*Rat*
Sat **8**	**Good for:** grand opening, business, contracts *Bad for: ground digging, fix house*	*Ox*
Sun **9**	**Good for:** most activities *Bad for: burial*	*Tiger*
Mon **10**	**Good for:** most activities *Bad for: ground digging, fix house*	*Rabbit*
Tue **11**	⚊ **DON'T DO IMPORTANT THINGS** ⚊	*Dragon*
Wed **12**	**Good for:** worship, prayer, planting *Bad for: most activities*	*Snake*
Thu **13**	⚊ **DON'T DO IMPORTANT THINGS** ⚊	*Horse*
Fri **14**	**Good for:** worship, prayer *Bad for: most activities*	*Sheep*
Sat **15**	**Good for:** most activities *Bad for: ground digging, fix house*	*Monkey*

Sun **16**	**Good for:** most activities *Bad for: burial*	*Rooster*
Mon **17**	**Good for:** prayer *Bad for: most activities*	*Dog*
Tue **18**	⊖ **DON'T DO IMPORTANT THINGS** ⊖	*Pig*
Wed **19**	**Good for:** most activities *Bad for: burial, ground digging*	*Rat*
Thu **20**	**Good for:** business, grand opening, contracts *Bad for: burial, lawsuit*	*Ox*
Fri **21**	**Good for:** worship, prayer *Bad for: most activities*	*Tiger*
Sat **22**	**Good for:** prayer, school *Bad for: most activities*	*Rabbit*
Sun **23**	⊖ **DON'T DO IMPORTANT THINGS** ⊖	*Dragon*
Mon **24**	⊖ **DON'T DO IMPORTANT THINGS** ⊖	*Snake*
Tue **25**	⊖ **DON'T DO IMPORTANT THINGS** ⊖	*Horse*
Wed **26**	**Good for:** prayer, worship *Bad for: most activities*	*Sheep*
Thu **27**	**Good for:** most activities *Bad for: ground digging, fix house*	*Monkey*
Fri **28**	**Good for:** most activities *Bad for: burial, ground digging*	*Rooster*
Sat **29**	**Good for:** most activities *Bad for: lawsuit*	*Dog*
Sun **30**	⊖ **DON'T DO IMPORTANT THINGS** ⊖	*Pig*

December 2014

Mon **1**	**Good for:** prayer, school **Bad for:** *most activities*	Rat
Tue **2**	**Good for:** most activities **Bad for:** *lawsuit, fix house*	Ox
Wed **3**	**Good for:** prayer **Bad for:** *most activities*	Tiger
Thu **4**	**Good for:** most activities **Bad for:** *funeral, ground digging*	Rabbit
Fri **5**	⊖ **DON'T DO IMPORTANT THINGS** ⊖	Dragon
Sat **6**	**Good for:** prayer, school **Bad for:** *most activities*	Snake
Sun **7**	⊖ **DON'T DO IMPORTANT THINGS** ⊖	Horse
Mon **8**	**Good for:** wedding, grand opening, contracts **Bad for:** *funeral, ground digging*	Sheep
Tue **9**	**Good for:** grand opening, contracts, business **Bad for:** *lawsuit*	Monkey
Wed **10**	**Good for:** prayer, school **Bad for:** *most activities*	Rooster
Thu **11**	**Good for:** most activities **Bad for:** *lawsuit, fix house*	Dog
Fri **12**	**Good for:** worship, prayer **Bad for:** *most activities*	Pig
Sat **13**	**Good for:** prayer **Bad for:** *most activities*	Rat
Sun **14**	⊖ **DON'T DO IMPORTANT THINGS** ⊖	Ox
Mon **15**	**Good for:** grand opening, contracts, business **Bad for:** *burial, ground digging*	Tiger

Day	Details	Zodiac
Tue **16**	**Good for:** prayer, school *Bad for: most activities*	*Rabbit*
Wed **17**	**Good for:** grand opening, contracts, business *Bad for: lawsuit, fix house*	*Dragon*
Thu **18**	**Good for:** worship, prayer *Bad for: most activities*	*Snake*
Fri **19**	● **DON'T DO IMPORTANT THINGS** ●	*Horse*
Sat **20**	**Good for:** prayer, school, contracts *Bad for: ground breaking, ground digging*	*Sheep*
Sun **21**	**Good for:** contracts, business *Bad for: lawsuit, fix house, grand opening*	*Monkey*
Mon **22**	**Good for:** worship, prayer *Bad for: most activities*	*Rooster*
Tue **23**	**Good for:** most activities *Bad for: lawsuit, fix house*	*Dog*
Wed **24**	**Good for:** worship, prayer, ground breaking *Bad for: most activities*	*Pig*
Thu **25**	**Good for:** worship, prayer *Bad for: most activities*	*Rat*
Fri **26**	**Good for:** prayer, school *Bad for: most activities*	*Ox*
Sat **27**	**Good for:** most activities *Bad for: funeral, ground digging*	*Tiger*
Sun **28**	**Good for:** worship, prayer *Bad for: most activities*	*Rabbit*
Mon **29**	**Good for:** worship, ground breaking, burial *Bad for: fix house*	*Dragon*
Tue **30**	**Good for:** worship, prayer, planting *Bad for: most activities*	*Snake* 12
Wed **31**	● **DON'T DO IMPORTANT THINGS** ●	*Horse*

January 2015

Day	Activities	Zodiac
Thu 1	**Good for:** most activities ***Bad for:*** *planting, fix house*	*Sheep*
Fri 2	**Good for:** grand opening, contracts, business ***Bad for:*** *ground breaking, ground digging*	*Monkey*
Sat 3	**Good for:** worship, prayer ***Bad for:*** *most activities*	*Rooster*
Sun 4	**Good for:** worship, prayer ***Bad for:*** *business, contracts*	*Dog*
Mon 5	**Good for:** worship ***Bad for:*** *most activities*	*Pig*
Tue 6	**Good for:** worship, prayer ***Bad for:*** *most activities*	*Rat*
Wed 7	⊖ **DON'T DO IMPORTANT THINGS** ⊖	*Ox*
Thu 8	**Good for:** most activities ***Bad for:*** *ground breaking, ground digging*	*Tiger*
Fri 9	**Good for:** wedding, grand opening, contracts ***Bad for:*** *funeral, ground digging*	*Rabbit*
Sat 10	**Good for:** worship, prayer ***Bad for:*** *most activities*	*Dragon*
Sun 11	**Good for:** worship, prayer, planting ***Bad for:*** *most activities*	*Snake*
Mon 12	⊖ **DON'T DO IMPORTANT THINGS** ⊖	*Horse*
Tue 13	**Good for:** worship, prayer ***Bad for:*** *most activities*	*Sheep*
Wed 14	**Good for:** most activities ***Bad for:*** *funeral, ground digging*	*Monkey*
Thu 15	**Good for:** worship, prayer, planting ***Bad for:*** *most activities*	*Rooster*

Fri 16	⊖ **DON'T DO IMPORTANT THINGS** ⊖	*Dog*
Sat 17	**Good for:** most activities ***Bad for:*** *funeral, ground digging*	*Pig*
Sun 18	**Good for:** worship, prayer ***Bad for:*** *most activities*	*Rat*
Mon 19	⊖ **DON'T DO IMPORTANT THINGS** ⊖	*Ox*
Tue 20	**Good for:** worship, prayer, planting ***Bad for:*** *business, buy property*	*Tiger*
Wed 21	**Good for:** most activities ***Bad for:*** *funeral, burial*	*Rabbit*
Thu 22	**Good for:** worship, prayer ***Bad for:*** *most activities*	*Dragon*
Fri 23	**Good for:** worship, school, planting ***Bad for:*** *most activities*	*Snake*
Sat 24	⊖ **DON'T DO IMPORTANT THINGS** ⊖	*Horse*
Sun 25	**Good for:** most activities ***Bad for:*** *burial, ground digging*	*Sheep*
Mon 26	**Good for:** worship, prayer ***Bad for:*** *most activities*	*Monkey*
Tue 27	**Good for:** worship, prayer, planting ***Bad for:*** *most activities*	*Rooster*
Wed 28	**Good for:** worship, prayer ***Bad for:*** *most activities*	*Dog*
Thu 29	**Good for:** begin mission, contracts, planting ***Bad for:*** *fix house, moving, lawsuit*	*Pig*
Fri 30	**Good for:** worship, prayer ***Bad for:*** *most activities*	*Rat*
Sat 31	⊖ **DON'T DO IMPORTANT THINGS** ⊖	*Ox*

幸福不是靠你的位高权重
而是靠你如何
自处之

It is not your position
that makes you happy
or unhappy,
it is your disposition

Calligraphy by Larry Sang

TEN THOUSAND YEAR CALENDAR

TEN-THOUSAND YEAR CALENDAR

	1ST MONTH Bing Yin	2ND MONTH Ding Mao	3RD MONTH Wu Chen	4TH MONTH Ji Si	5TH MONTH Geng Wu	6TH MONTH Xin Wei	
1	1/31 Ren Yin	3/1 Xin Wei	3/31 Xin Chou	4/29 Geng Wu	5/29 Geng Zi	6/27 Ji Si	1
2	2/1 Gui Mao	3/2 Ren Shen	4/1 Ren Yin	4/30 Xin Wei	5/30 Xin Chou	6/28 Geng Wu	2
3	2/2 Jia Chen	3/3 Gui You	4/2 Gui Mao	5/1 Ren Shen	5/31 Ren Yin	6/29 Xin Wei	3
4	2/3 Yi Si	3/4 Jia Xu	4/3 Jia Chen	5/2 Gui You	6/1 Gui Mao	6/30 Ren Shen	4
5	2/4 Bing Wu	3/5 Yi Hai	4/4 Yi Si	5/3 Jia Xu	6/2 Jia Chen	7/1 Gui You	5
6	2/5 Ding Wei	3/6 Bing Zi	4/5 Bing Wu	5/4 Yi Hai	6/3 Yi Si	7/2 Jia Xu	6
7	2/6 Wu Shen	3/7 Ding Chou	4/6 Ding Wei	5/5 Bing Zi	6/4 Bing Wu	7/3 Yi Hai	7
8	2/7 Ji You	3/8 Wu Yin	4/7 Wu Shen	5/6 Ding Chou	6/5 Ding Wei	7/4 Bing Zi	8
9	2/8 Geng Xu	3/9 Ji Mao	4/8 Ji You	5/7 Wu Yin	6/6 Wu Shen	7/5 Ding Chou	9
10	2/9 Xin Hai	3/10 Geng Chen	4/9 Geng Xu	5/8 Ji Mao	6/7 Ji You	7/6 Wu Yin	10
11	2/10 Ren Zi	3/11 Xin Si	4/10 Xin Hai	5/9 Geng Chen	6/8 Geng Xu	7/7 Ji Mao	11
12	2/11 Gui Chou	3/12 Ren Wu	4/11 Ren Zi	5/10 Xin Si	6/9 Xin Hai	7/8 Geng Chen	12
13	2/12 Jia Yin	3/13 Gui Wei	4/12 Gui Chou	5/11 Ren Wu	6/10 Ren Zi	7/9 Xin Si	13
14	2/13 Yi Mao	3/14 Jia Shen	4/13 Jia Yin	5/12 Gui Wei	6/11 Gui Chou	7/10 Ren Wu	14
15	2/14 Bing Chen	3/15 Yi You	4/14 Yi Mao	5/13 Jia Shen	6/12 Jia Yin	7/11 Gui Wei	15
16	2/15 Ding Si	3/16 Bing Xu	4/15 Bing Chen	5/14 Yi You	6/13 Yi Mao	7/12 Jia Shen	16
17	2/16 Wu Wu	3/17 Ding Hai	4/16 Ding Si	5/15 Bing Xu	6/14 Bing Chen	7/13 Yi You	17
18	2/17 Ji Wei	3/18 Wu Zi	4/17 Wu Wu	5/16 Ding Hai	6/15 Ding Si	7/14 Bing Xu	18
19	2/18 Geng Shen	3/19 Ji Chou	4/18 Ji Wei	5/17 Wu Zi	6/16 Wu Wu	7/15 Ding Hai	19
20	2/19 Xin You	3/20 Geng Yin	4/19 Geng Shen	5/18 Ji Chou	6/17 Ji Wei	7/16 Wu Zi	20
21	2/20 Ren Xu	3/21 Xin Mao	4/20 Xin You	5/19 Geng Yin	6/18 Geng Shen	7/17 Ji Chou	21
22	2/21 Gui Hai	3/22 Ren Chen	4/21 Ren Xu	5/20 Xin Mao	6/19 Xin You	7/18 Geng Yin	22
23	2/22 Jia Zi	3/23 Gui Si	4/22 Gui Hai	5/21 Ren Chen	6/20 Ren Xu	7/19 Xin Mao	23
24	2/23 Yi Chou	3/24 Jia Wu	4/23 Jia Zi	5/22 Gui Si	6/21 Gui Hai	7/20 Ren Chen	24
25	2/24 Bing Yin	3/25 Yi Wei	4/24 Yi Chou	5/23 Jia Wu	6/22 Jia Zi	7/21 Gui Si	25
26	2/25 Ding Mao	3/26 Bing Shen	4/25 Bing Yin	5/24 Yi Wei	6/23 Yi Chou	7/22 Jia Wu	26
27	2/26 Wu Chen	3/27 Ding You	4/26 Ding Mao	5/25 Bing Shen	6/24 Bing Yin	7/23 Yi Wei	27
28	2/27 Ji Si	3/28 Wu Xu	4/27 Wu Chen	5/26 Ding You	6/25 Ding Mao	7/24 Bing Shen	28
29	2/28 Geng Wu	3/29 Ji Hai	4/28 Ji Si	5/27 Wu Xu	6/26 Wu Chen	7/25 Ding You	29
30		3/30 Geng Zi		5/28 Ji Hai		7/26 Wu Xu	30

	8 White	7 Red	6 White	5 Yellow	4 Green	3 Jade	
Jie	Li Chun 2/4 6:21am	Jing Zhi 3/6 12:07am	Qing Ming 4/5 4:54am	Li Xia 5/5 10:16pm	Mang Zhong 6/6 2:32am	Xiao Shu 7/7 12:57pm	Jie
Qi	Yu Shui 2/19 2:04am	Chun Fen 3/21 12:57am	Gu Yu 4/20 12:12pm	Xiao Man 5/21 12:17pm	Xia Zhi 6/21 7:21pm	Da Shu 7/23 6:27am	Qi

Year: Jia Wu • 4 Green  2014

	7TH MONTH Ren Shen	8TH MONTH Gui You	9TH MONTH Jia Xu	LEAP MONTH	10TH MONTH Yi Hai	11TH MONTH Bing Zi	12TH MONTH Ding Chou	
1	7/27 Ji Hai	8/25 Wu Chen	9/24 Wu Xu	10/24 Wu Chen	11/22 Ding You	2014 - 2015 12/22 Ding Mao	1/20 Bing Shen	1
2	7/28 Geng Zi	8/26 Ji Si	9/25 Ji Hai	10/25 Ji Si	11/23 Wu Xu	12/23 Wu Chen	1/21 Ding You	2
3	7/29 Xin Chou	8/27 Geng Wu	9/26 Geng Zi	10/26 Geng Wu	11/24 Ji Hai	12/24 Ji Si	1/22 Wu Xu	3
4	7/30 Ren Yin	8/28 Xin Wei	9/27 Xin Chou	10/27 Xin Wei	11/25 Geng Zi	12/25 Geng Wu	1/23 Ji Hai	4
5	7/31 Gui Mao	8/29 Ren Shen	9/28 Ren Yin	10/28 Ren Shen	11/26 Xin Chou	12/26 Xin Wei	1/24 Geng Zi	5
6	8/1 Jia Chen	8/30 Gui You	9/29 Gui Mao	10/29 Gui You	11/27 Ren Yin	12/27 Ren Shen	1/25 Xin Chou	6
7	8/2 Yi Si	8/31 Jia Xu	9/30 Jia Chen	10/30 Jia Xu	11/28 Gui Mao	12/28 Gui You	1/26 Ren Yin	7
8	8/3 Bing Wu	9/1 Yi Hai	10/1 Yi Si	10/31 Yi Hai	11/29 Jia Chen	12/29 Jia Xu	1/27 Gui Mao	8
9	8/4 Ding Wei	9/2 Bing Zi	10/2 Bing Wu	11/1 Bing Zi	11/30 Yi Si	12/30 Yi Hai	1/28 Jia Chen	9
10	8/5 Wu Shen	9/3 Ding Chou	10/3 Ding Wei	11/2 Ding Chou	12/1 Bing Wu	12/31 Bing Zi	1/29 Yi Si	10
11	8/6 Ji You	9/4 Wu Yin	10/4 Wu Shen	11/3 Wu Yin	12/2 Ding Wei	1/1 Ding Chou	1/30 Bing Wu	11
12	8/7 Geng Xu	9/5 Ji Mao	10/5 Ji You	11/4 Ji Mao	12/3 Wu Shen	1/2 Wu Yin	1/31 Ding Wei	12
13	8/8 Xin Hai	9/6 Geng Chen	10/6 Geng Xu	11/5 Geng Chen	12/4 Ji You	1/3 Ji Mao	2/1 Wu Shen	13
14	8/9 Ren Zi	9/7 Xin Si	10/7 Xin Hai	11/6 Xin Si	12/5 Geng Xu	1/4 Geng Chen	2/2 Ji You	14
15	8/10 Gui Chou	9/8 Ren Wu	10/8 Ren Zi	11/7 Ren Wu	12/6 Xin Hai	1/5 Xin Si	2/3 Geng Xu	15
16	8/11 Jia Yin	9/9 Gui Wei	10/9 Gui Chou	11/8 Gui Wei	12/7 Ren Zi	1/6 Ren Wu	2/4 Xin Hai	16
17	8/12 Yi Mao	9/10 Jia Shen	10/10 Jia Yin	11/9 Jia Shen	12/8 Gui Chou	1/7 Gui Wei	2/5 Ren Zi	17
18	8/13 Bing Chen	9/11 Yi You	10/11 Yi Mao	11/10 Yi You	12/9 Jia Yin	1/8 Jia Shen	2/6 Gui Chou	18
19	8/14 Ding Si	9/12 Bing Xu	10/12 Bing Chen	11/11 Bing Xu	12/10 Yi Mao	1/9 Yi You	2/7 Jia Yin	19
20	8/15 Wu Wu	9/13 Ding Hai	10/13 Ding Si	11/12 Ding Hai	12/11 Bing Chen	1/10 Bing Xu	2/8 Yi Mao	20
21	8/16 Ji Wei	9/14 Wu Zi	10/14 Wu Wu	11/13 Wu Zi	12/12 Ding Si	1/11 Ding Hai	2/9 Bing Chen	21
22	8/17 Geng Shen	9/15 Ji Chou	10/15 Ji Wei	11/14 Ji Chou	12/13 Wu Wu	1/12 Wu Zi	2/10 Ding Si	22
23	8/18 Xin You	9/16 Geng Yin	10/16 Geng Shen	11/15 Geng Yin	12/14 Ji Wei	1/13 Ji Chou	2/11 Wu Wu	23
24	8/19 Ren Xu	9/17 Xin Mao	10/17 Xin You	11/16 Xin Mao	12/15 Geng Shen	1/14 Geng Yin	2/12 Ji Wei	24
25	8/20 Gui Hai	9/18 Ren Chen	10/18 Ren Xu	11/17 Ren Chen	12/16 Xin You	1/15 Xin Mao	2/13 Geng Shen	25
26	8/21 Jia Zi	9/19 Gui Si	10/19 Gui Hai	11/18 Gui Si	12/17 Ren Xu	1/16 Ren Chen	2/14 Xin You	26
27	8/22 Yi Chou	9/20 Jia Wu	10/20 Jia Zi	11/19 Jia Wu	12/18 Gui Hai	1/17 Gui Si	2/15 Ren Xu	27
28	8/23 Bing Yin	9/21 Yi Wei	10/21 Yi Chou	11/20 Yi Wei	12/19 Jia Zi	1/18 Jia Wu	2/16 Gui Hai	28
29	8/24 Ding Mao	9/22 Bing Shen	10/22 Bing Yin	11/21 Bing Shen	12/20 Yi Chou	1/19 Yi Wei	2/17 Jia Zi	29
30		9/23 Ding You	10/23 Ding Mao		12/21 Bing Yin		2/18 Yi Chou	30
	2 Black	1 White	9 Purple		8 White	7 Red	6 White	
Jie	Li Qiu 8/7 11:02pm	Bai Lu 9/8 2:21am	Han Lu 10/8 6:20pm		Li Dong 11/7 9:36pm	Da Xue 12/7 2:11pm	Xiao Han 1/6 12:57am	Jie
Qi	Chu Shu 8/23 1:53pm	Qiu Fen 9/23 11:51am	Shuang Jiang 10/23 9:30pm		Xiao Xue 11/22 6:58pm	Dong Zhi 12/22 7:50am	Da Han 1/20 6:05pm	Qi

The Principles of Feng Shui - Book One

After years of intensive research, experimentation, exploration and teaching of Feng Shui, Master Larry Sang put forth his accumulated knowledge and insights into this book. This book will systematically introduce Feng Shui to its readers. This book is recommended for our Beginning, Intermediate and Advanced Feng Shui classes.

Available in paperback and ebook. $18.75 US

Sang's Luopan

The Luopan is a Chinese compass used in Feng Shui readings. It offers more information for a Feng Shui reading besides the cardinal and inter-cardinal directions. Whereas a Western compass may be used in Feng Shui, a Luopan saves several steps in calculation. The Luopan is 4 inches (10cm) square. The Luopan is recommended for user in our Feng Shui classes and practice.

$60.00 US

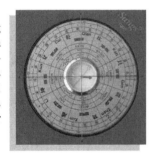

Yi Jing for Love and Marriage

In the journey of life, we often experience times of doubt, confusion and feeling lost. What should we do when facing this type of situation? The Changing Hexagram Divination method can help by predicting what may happen. It can provide guidelines for coping with difficult situations or insight into beneficial ones. This book provides a simple method for the reader to predict the answers to their questions and to help others. Besides resolving confusion and doubt, it also provides a fun hobby for those interested in the ancient art of divination. Use this book as your consultant on Love and Marriage when the need arises!

Available in paperback and ebook. $14.75 US

Ten-Thousand Year Calendar (1882 - 2031)

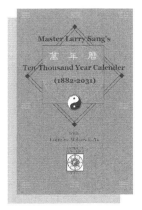

Normally printed in Chinese, but now in English, this handy reference guide is what the Chinese call the Ten-Thousand Year Calendar. This calendar contains information for 150 years, from 1882 to 2031. It gives the annual, monthly, and daily stem and branch, the annual and monthly flying star, as well as the lunar day of the month. It also gives information about the lunar and solar months, the solstices, equinoxes, and the beginning of the four seasons in the Chinese calendar. The Ten-Thousand Year Calendar is used for Feng Shui, Chinese Astrology, Day Selection, and various predictive techniques.

Available in ebook only. $26.00 US

Feng Shui Facts and Myths

This book is a collection of stories about Feng Shui and Astrology. Master Sang attempts to explain aspects of Feng Shui and Chinese Astrology, as the terms are understood or misunderstood in the West. This book will provide you with deeper information on the Chinese culture traditions of Feng Shui and Astrology.

Available in paperback and ebook. $16.00 US

Larry Sang's
2014 Chinese Astrology & Feng Shui Guide
The Year of The Horse

Each section explains how to determine the key piece: determining your animal sign; how to read the Feng Shui of your home; and how to read the Day Selection calendar - a valuable day by day indication of favorable and unfavorable activity.

Available in paperback and ebook. $14.75 US

COURSE CATALOG

The following is a current list of the courses available from *The American Feng Shui Institute.* Please consult our online catalog for course fees, descriptions and new additions.

FENG SHUI

CLASS	CLASS NAME	PREREQUISITE
FS095	Introduction to Feng Shui	
FS101/OL	Beginning Feng Shui & Online	-
FS102/OL	Intermediate Feng Shui & Online	-
FS201/OL	Advanced Feng Shui & Online	FS101+FS102/OL
FS205/OL	Advanced Sitting and Facing & Online	FS101+FS102/OL
FS106/OL	Additional Concepts on Sitting & Facing	FS102/OL
FS225	Feng Shui Folk Beliefs	FS201
FS227/OL	Professional Skills for Feng Shui Consultants	FS201
FS231	Feng Shui Yourself & Your Business	FS201
FS235	Symptoms of a House	FS201
FS250	Explanation of Advanced Feng Shui Theories	FS201
FS275	9 Palace Grid and Pie Chart Graph Usage & Online	FS201
FS280	Advanced East West Theory	FS201
FS301	Advanced Feng Shui Case Study 1 & 2	FS201
FS303	Advanced Feng Shui Case Study 3 & 4 + Online	FS201
FS305/OL	Advanced Feng Shui Case Study 5 & Online	FS201
FS306/OL	Advanced Feng Shui Case Study 6 & Online	FS201
FS307/OL	Advanced Feng Shui Case Study 7 & Online	FS201
FS308/OL	Advanced Feng Shui Case Study 8 & Online	FS201
FS309	Advanced Feng Shui Case Study 9 & 10	FS201
FS311	Advanced Feng Shui Case Study 11	FS201
FS312/OL	Advanced Feng Shui Case Study 12	FS201
FS313/OL	Advanced Feng Shui Case Study 13 & Online	FS201 & AS101
FS314	Advanced Feng Shui Case Study 14	FS201
FS315	Advanced Feng Shui Case Study 15	FS201
FS316/FS317	Advanced Feng Shui Case Study 16 & 17	FS201
FS318/FS319	Advanced Feng Shui Case Study 18 & 19	FS201
FS320/FS321	Advanced Feng Shui Case Study 20 & 21	FS201
FS322/FS323	Advanced Feng Shui Case Study 22 & 23	FS201 & AS101
FS324/FS325	Advanced Feng Shui Case Study 24 & 25	FS201
FS326/FS327	Advanced Feng Shui Case Study 26 & 27	FS201

FENG SHUI - *continued from previous page*

FS340/OL	Secrets of the Five Ghosts	FS201
FS341	The Secrets of the "San Ban Gua"	FS201
FS260/OL	Lawsuit Support & Online	FS201 & AS101
FS270/OL	The Taisui, Year Breaker, Three Sha & Online	FS201 & AS101
FS350/OL	Feng Shui Day Selection 1 & Online	FS201 & AS101
FS351/OL	Feng Shui Day Selection 2 & Online	FS201 & FS350/OL
FS360/OL	Marriage and Life Partner Selection Online	FS201 & AS101
FS375/OL	Introduction to Yin House Feng Shui	FS201

YI JING

YJ101	Beginning Yi Jing Divination	AS101
YJ102	Yi Jing Coin Divination	AS101
YJ103	Plum Flower Yi Jing Calculation	AS101

CHINESE ASTROLOGY

AS101	Stems and Branches & Online	-
AS102	Four Pillars 1 & 2 (Zi Ping Ba Zi)	AS101 or AS101/OL
AS103	Four Pillars 3 & 4 (Zi Ping Ba Zi)	AS102
AS105	Four Pillars 5 & 6 (Zi Ping Ba Zi)	AS103
AS201A/OL	Beginning Zi Wei Dou Shu, Part 1	AS101
AS201B/OL	Beginning Zi Wei Dou Shu, Part 2	AS201A/OL
AS211/OL	Intermediate Zi Wei Dou Shu	AS201B/OL
AS301A/OL	Advanced Zi Wei Dou Shu, Part 1	AS211/OL
AS301B/OL	Advanced Zi Wei Dou Shu, Part 2	AS201A/OL
AS311/OL	Zi Wei Dou Shu Case Study 1 & Online	AS301B/OL
AS313/OL	Zi Wei Dou Shu Case Study 3 & Online	AS301B/OL
AS314	Zi Wei Dou Shu Case Study 2 & 4	AS301B/OL

CHINESE ARTS

CA101/OL	Palm & Face Reading 1 & 2	-
CA102	Palm & Face Reading 3 & 4	CA101 or CA101/OL
CA103	Palm & Face Reading for Health	-
CA121	Introduction to Chinese Medicine	-
CA110	Professional Face Reading	-

CHINESE PHILOSOPHY

CP101	Introduction to Daode Jing	-
CP102	Feng Shui Yourself	-

CLASSES AT THE
AMERICAN FENG SHUI INSTITUTE

Due to the limited seating capacity, reservations are necessary and seats are on a first come first serve basis. To reserve your seat, a $50.00 US deposit is required and is non-refundable if cancellation by student takes place less than three days before class. Please mail-in check or call us to reserve your seat with a credit card*. Balance is due on the first day of class.

Please DO NOT e-mail credit card information as this is not a secure method

ONLINE CLASSES WITH THE
AMERICAN FENG SHUI INSTITUTE FEATURE:

- Easy navigation
- Self tests at the end of each module
- A discussion board with trained Institute's Instructors
- Audio clips for pronunciation
- An online discussion board
- An instant feedback final exam

The online classes are self-paced study modules. They are segmented into four, one-week lessons that lead you at your own pace, over the four-week course. You have 60 days to complete the course work.

For more information, please see our website:
www.amfengshui.com

AMERICAN
FENG SHUI

INSTITUTE

7220 N. Rosemead Blvd.
Suite. 204
San Gabriel, CA 91775
Phone: (626) 571-2757
E-mail: fsinfo@amfengshui.com

AS A STUDENT OF
THE AMERICAN FENG SHUI INSTITUTE:

You will receive a certificate of completion from the American Feng Shui Institute, for the Beginning/Intermediate and Advanced Feng Shui Classes. Please do not confuse this certification as licensing, as there are no requirements for practitioner at this time.

As a student of the Institute, we are available to assist you with your studies. We have an online Bulletin Board for questions and answers, featuring a topic search. You will obtain access to the Bulletin Board upon completion of the Advance Feng Shui class. Due to the complexity of the courses, graduates may repeat in the classroom that you have already taken, pending available seats. Please see our online course catalog for the most current course offerings.

CANCELLATION AND REFUND POLICY:

All institutional charges shall be returned to the registrant less a $50.00 US cancellation fee, if cancellation notice is received prior to or on the first day of instruction. Any notification of withdrawal or cancellation and any request for a refund are required to be made in writing.

Refunds shall be made within thirty (30) days of receipt of the withdrawal or cancellation notice and refund request.

The institute does not participate in the Student Tuition Recovery Fund (STRF). We are registered with the State of California. Registration means we have met certain minimum standards imposed by the state for registered schools on the basis of our written application to the state. Registration does not mean we have met all of the more extensive standards required by the state for schools that are approved to operate or license or that the state has verified the information we submitted with our registration form.